What others are saying about ...

A Firm GRASP

"In an online world full of competing noise, it's no wonder that most of us struggle to be noticed. Susan's book does an exceptional job at sharing the truth behind this God-given desire, how it is often manipulated, and how the God-of-mercy fills this space. Her real-life relatable stories and deep understanding of the psychological and spiritual needs of women with purpose, provides the needed anchor to no longer vacillate between insecurity and confidence in the call. This is a book to sit with and soak up, bits at a time, until all that is left is a firm grasp in the One who has always seen you."

—**Tiffany Jo Baker,** speaker, strategizer, author and podcast host of All The Things TV

"Susan Hoekstra offers an honest look at our profound desire for affirmation and the temptations we face when we feel undervalued. She acknowledges the unfortunate reality of being insecure but also provides the hopeful reassurance that God's loving attention can meet our every longing."

— **Angie Baughman,** Pastor and Founder, Steady On Ministries

"When I first began working in behavioral health, over time it became apparent to me that the world and the enemy use two key ideas to keep people—believers and unbelievers alike—stuck. One, there's something wrong with you; and two, God's holding out on you.

If we believe those lies, then we will constantly cap our lives and what we are capable of. Not because we aren't capable, but because the stories we come to tell ourselves about ourselves lead us to that conclusion. "I'm not loveable, money's hard to make, it works for others, but not for me..." The fruit of these lies is a self-limited life where no amounts of affirmations or wishful thinking will get us unstuck. Only truth makes us free. Period.

In *A Firm GRASP*, Susan leans into our desire for validation and affirmation, giving her readers permission to confront their own sense of unworthiness. Offering wonderful insights for where to find the truth of our own tremendous value and worth in God's finished work at the cross, we're encouraged to stop dwelling on what's wrong with us. Instead of feeling like our desire for validation and affirmation is somehow an indication of brokenness, Susan shares how, through her own powerful journey, we can let go of the lies we default to, move forward into the reality of who God says we are, and *truly* embrace God's work at the cross, validating both our longing for redemption while affirming that we are, in truth, worthy of it."

—**Grant Porteous,** MSW, PCF, Founder of Grant Porteous Coaching

"Susan takes us on an important and courageous journey helping us navigate our need for affirmation. There are healthy and unhealthy ways to satisfy this appetite we all have. What makes her work meaningful is how she helps place God as our guide to help us navigate the waters of self-awareness. So, if you ever struggle to "love yourself"—consider this book to help clarify your path forward."

—**Ben Snyder,** Lead Pastor, Cedar Creek Church

"I have known Susan for years. Our relationship started with me facilitating a class she was a part of. When I met Susan, I saw a woman that felt defeated. As time went on, I was blessed to see her letting go and letting God take the helm and guide her through a hard but very positive new season in her life. Watching her go from a woman without hope to a woman that knew God had a wonderful plan for her was so awesome! Her goal in life now is to disciple women and use her testimony for the glory of God! I am so blessed to have her call me friend. This book is an outpouring of her testimony and commitment to disciple others."

—**Lisa Lempke,** Northwest Michigan Jesus Ministry

"As a worship pastor and musician for many years, I've often been tempted to leverage my leadership as a platform for my own validation and affirmation. I'm guessing I'm not the only one. The "attaboys" and pats on the back ultimately fall short of our true heart's desire that only the God of mercy can fill. I wish I would have had Susan's book many years ago to help me process what I was feeling, why I was feeling it, and ultimately how to embrace with a "firm grasp" the incredible remedy that's available to all."

—**Adam Dennis,** Worship Pastor, Lifepoint Bible Church

"Susan Hoekstra is the real deal. After watching how she leads her own life, and how she shepherds and pours into others, I couldn't wait to read her well-researched thoughts on getting "a firm grasp" on our God-given identity. This multi-talented woman—professional musician, academic, author, church leader, lay counselor, and podcaster—is characteristically vulnerable and real about her own struggles as she explores what it means to find true significance in a "notice-me" world. She roots her points deeply in Scripture and seasons them with her trademark humor and compassion. Whether you know it or not, you need *A Firm GRASP* to help you understand our deep human need for acknowledgment and affirmation, and where we will ultimately find that need met. This book is transforming."

—**Anne Cody,** Director of Groups, Trinity Church

©2021 Susan Hoekstra

All rights reserved. No portion of this book may be reproduced or transmitted in any form or by any means—electronic, mechanical, photocopy, recording, scanning, or other—except for brief quotations in critical reviews, or articles without the permission of the author.

ISBN: 978-0-578-89062-3

Unless otherwise noted, Scripture quotations are from The ESV® Bible (The Holy Bible, English Standard Version®), copyright © 2001 by Crossway, a publishing ministry of Good News Publishers. Used by permission. All rights reserved.

Cover design and interior formatting by Nelly Murariu at PixBeeDesign.com

A Firm GRASP

*Feeling Validated in a
Notice-Me World*

SUSAN HOEKSTRA

To those who have validated or affirmed me through the mercy of God, I thank you.

To those I have failed to offer the mercy of God, I apologize

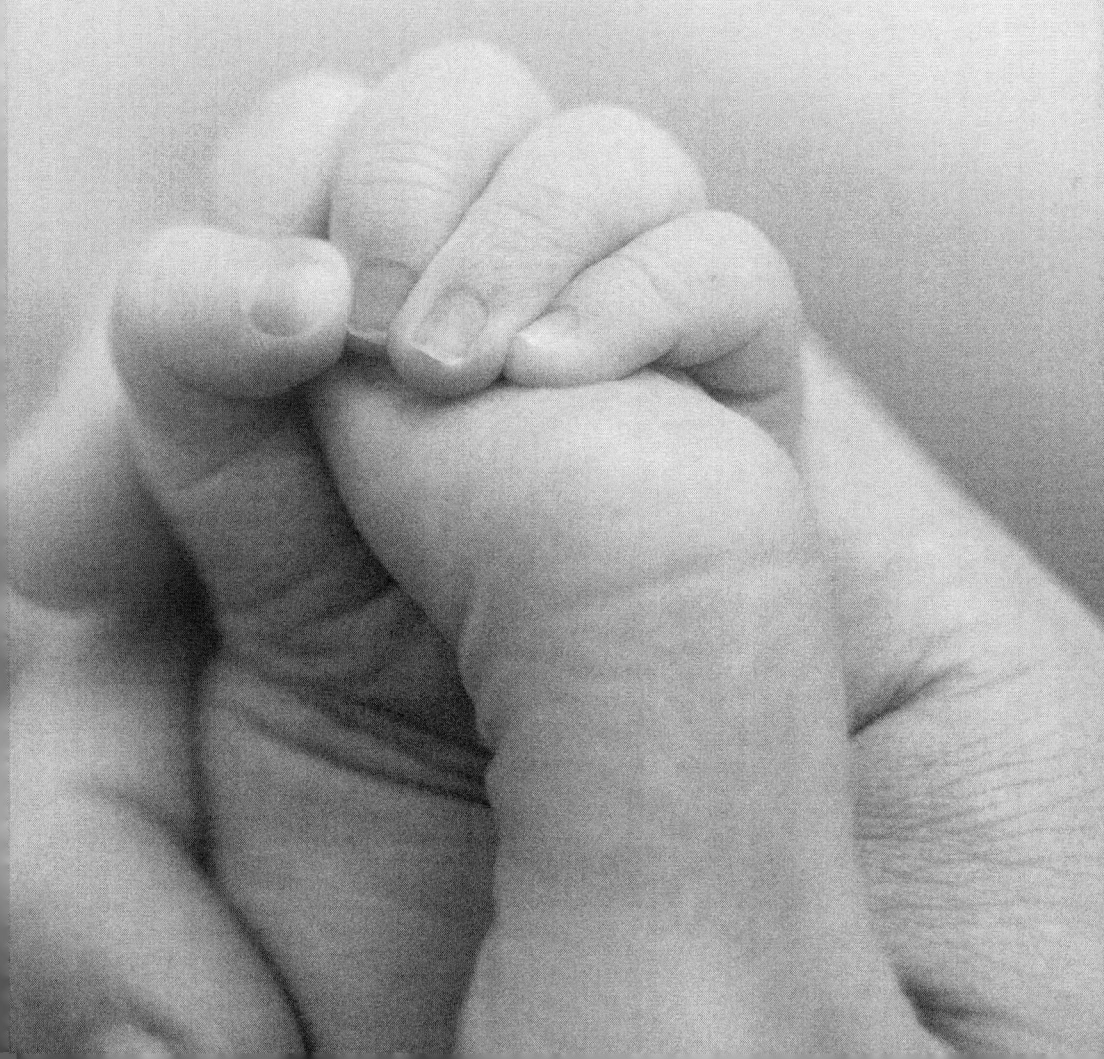

ACKNOWLEDGMENTS

*Thus, says the Lord, the God of Israel,
"Write all the words which I have
spoken to you in a book."*
—**Psalm 45:1**

Writing a book is like running a marathon. Once you make the decision, a training period begins. Each chapter becomes a mile or two, the editing another. I've asked myself multiple times, "Why write a book"? As I came to peace regarding this project, my passion turned to burden.

Friends, there are people out there hurting because they don't feel validated. Maybe that person is you. Perhaps as a child you were neglected, criticized, or experienced abuse. Maybe you're creative yet feel unnoticed. You're not alone. All of us need an eyewitness to our life. This book is because of you. This book is FOR you.

I'm also grateful for the validation and affirmation which beautifully came to me from God through others. You know who you are. From my friend Terri, the first person I shared this book idea with, to editors, publishers, family, friends, fellow writers and musicians, church family, podcast listeners, and prayer warriors, I can't thank you enough for your support.

A special thanks to my husband Dick, the president of my fan club, who patiently listened and validated my daily ramblings. This book wouldn't have happened without all you do behind the scenes. Together, we have seen God take notice. I look forward to sharing stories of what God has done once He's coached us to cross that finish line. To God be the glory!

CONTENTS

Introduction	xiii
Chapter 1 – The Handshake	1
Chapter 2 – Give and Take	13
Chapter 3 – Be Still	21
Chapter 4 – A Star is Born	31
Chapter 5 – The Fan Club	43
Chapter 6 – Facets	53
Chapter 7 – The Frame	65
Chapter 8 – Enter the Hall	75
Chapter 9 – The Vow	83
Chapter 10 – The Trap	91
Chapter 11 – Cramps	101
Chapter 12 – I—Dentity	111
Chapter 13 – The Seesaw	125
Chapter 14 – Offense or Defense	133
Chapter 15 – The Why	147
Chapter 16 – Selfies	157
Chapter 17 – Who's Listening?	167
Chapter 18 – Treat Yourself	177
Chapter 19 – Mercy Mode	187
Chapter 20 – Safety Net	197
Chapter 21 – Embrace	207
Chapter 22 – Masterpiece	215
Chapter 23 – The Master	223
Soaking Session for personal reflection	231
Life - Line Chart	232
Validation and Affirmation QUIZES	232
Reflective Questions	233
About the Author	257

INTRODUCTION

"

For my people have committed two evils:
they have forsaken me, the fountain of living waters,
and hewed out cisterns for themselves,
broken cisterns that can hold no water.
—Jeremiah 2:13

"You have no idea how bad my life is," he screamed in his loudest voice, which resonated throughout the dimly lit restaurant. As he passionately shared details of his failing marriage, financial struggles, ailing health, and recently deceased mother, others in the restaurant couldn't help but notice his overbearing countenance.

Minutes felt like hours as she desperately attempted to acknowledge his pain and temper his escalating volume. Exasperated, she finally whispered, "Okay, okay, even though you're not the only one who has problems, you win. I don't understand why you would want this award, but I concede. I officially award you—with glowing honors—the 'I Have the Worst Life' award.'"

Expecting the conversation to escalate, she was puzzled by his instant change of demeanor. As if by magic, he immediately calmed down. Confused, she couldn't help but ask herself what had happened. Were his experiences validated? Did he finally feel acknowledged?

Weeks later, she arrived at the newly built high school painted in blue and grey. The auditorium filled quickly with parents, grandparents, and friends, all eager to attend the Honors and Awards Ceremony. As she heard her daughter's name called for numerous awards, the pride radiating from her face was noticeable. How rewarding to see her daughter celebrated. She felt affirmed too.

It begins as early as a baby's cry. Toddlers seek attention through temper tantrums, teenagers through rebellious overtures, and twentysomethings with budding accomplishments. As we mature, we tend to disguise our need to be acknowledged or celebrated, but it's there every time we feel unappreciated. It's there when we have an excessive need for compliments, or demand affirmation when we haven't been acknowledged. It's especially there every time we look in the mirror and don't feel good enough.

Imagine a different life. Imagine a life where it's okay to admit your need without feeling selfish. Imagine a life where being acknowledged and celebrated satisfies, leaving you confident. By anchoring in God's mercy, you are excited for the next adventure.

While this kind of life is possible, unfortunately, it rarely happens. All too often, we live with a deficit. Without acknowledgment, we feel ignored. If no one affirms us, we feel we're not good enough. If we mess up, we feel unworthy.

A Firm GRASP addresses this discomfort, highlighting three areas. First, the book reveals our need for validation (acknowledgment) and affirmation (approval) and identifies any misconceptions or deficits we may have. Second, the book explores ways we may have responded to our deficit, encouraging self-awareness. Third, the book embraces a deeper understanding of mercy, giving us a firm grasp to create our masterpiece and fulfill the mission.

Introduction

Make no mistake about it, dear reader, this book encourages transformation. Before transformation can take place, we need to accept that change requires a transition. Your transition may get tough, it may be exhausting, but hang in there. God is in the transformation business! As you become more self-aware, I pray you'll embrace your before and after. Transformation is a lot like home renovations. We long for the end result, but there's a whole lot of work that happens before we get there.

I can't attempt to write a spiritual transformation book without sharing how God transformed me. It's complicated, but from day one, I've struggled with this feeling of not being good enough. My journey revealed how neglect, abuse, betrayal, envy, creative frustration, and fatherless experiences shaped who I am today. These experiences led me to seek satisfaction from other sources. I admit, I'm not an expert, but as I've experienced His transformation, God has given me the ability to see life through the lens of validation and affirmation. As you read my back story, I pray you will feel inspired about what God can do.

As a young child, I grew up in the racially tense streets of Detroit. Break-ins, drug dealers, and neighborhood fights were commonplace. I found myself in a number of unsafe situations, even when innocently playing games outside. For example, doesn't a girl long to remember her first kiss? Unfortunately, at age eight, three things happened. The first incident was when I was playing hide and seek. A sixteen-year-old boy wanted to be on my team, so we hid together. Imagine my surprise when he French kissed me. Being so young, I didn't know what to do and was too confused to tell anyone. Who was there to notice?

Later that year, at our local park, someone threatened me with a switchblade. Once I saw the knife, I jumped off the swing-set frightened, and immediately ran home. Fighting the uncomfortable feeling in the pit of my stomach, I tried to tell my Mom, but I failed to get her attention. Preoccupied, she wasn't emotionally available, so I chose to forget about it. Or at least, I put it in a box inside my head.

The same year I attended a subsidized summer camp for two weeks. This camp was for under privileged children in Detroit. While there, I was physically bullied by two of the girls in my cabin. They threatened to hurt me more if I told on them. All I learned was that tattle tailing is no way to make friends at camp.

Meanwhile, growing up with three older brothers with a chauvinistic Dad also proved to have its set of challenges. As the youngest and only girl, it was inevitable to feel unheard. It didn't help that Mom was a screamer. Her screaming fits were unpredictable and accompanied by her slipper. Because I was never given any explanation about what I did to deserve her slaps, I became confused, frightened, and apprehensive about the next blow-up. All the excess drama didn't leave her with enough self-awareness to recognize how her sensitive, overweight daughter experienced her. Was this how all families lived?

Next, there was Dad. Rheumatic fever plagued him as a child, causing severe heart problems. He suffered his first heart attack at twenty-seven. Berger's disease ate away his legs, resulting in one leg being amputated above the knee and the other below. Because of his health issues, many childhood hours were spent in hospital waiting rooms, feeling uncertain of our family's future. Couple that with his disabilities, and we couldn't do things other families did. One day, as I was watching Dad manage life in a wheelchair, I overheard him characterize himself as a 'misfit.' That day, that word, changed my entire concept of my Dad, my family—and of myself.

With medical bills piling up and Dad unable to work, our financial situation became bleak. Handouts, public assistance, and subsidized summer camps became our new normal. One winter night, the eve of Valentine's Day, when I was ten years old, I woke up to unusual

Introduction

sounds coming from my parent's bedroom. As I heard the panic in my Mom's voice, I sensed it was serious, so I clung to my blanket in fear. Played out like a scene in a movie, complete with fire trucks arriving and medical personnel administering life support, at age 39, Dad died of a heart attack.

After he passed, life changed. Working through feelings of grief and abandonment, I watched as our family unit dissolved. Mom was overwhelmed with work and raising three teenage boys. My brothers gravitated to various adventures outside of the home, including working at an early age. I did my best to be the 'good girl.' I did well in school and developed a strong interest in reading and music. Although Mom took me shopping, and taught me what she knew, more times than not, her overweight, insecure daughter with buck teeth, fell off her radar. Without adequate life skills, this single, grieving mom longed for companionship, financial stability, and a father figure in the home. And then it happened.

Not too long after Dad died, a prominent member of the community entered our life. At first, he seemed like a grandfather figure, visiting our family and offering much needed financial support. My brothers were usually busy working, so they didn't really get to know him. Mom seemed to enjoy her visits with him, but I didn't. For her, he was in a "higher social class," which made her feel important. For me, He made me uncomfortable. Maybe it was the twenty-dollar bills he would slip into my hand as he French-kissed me or the way he wanted me to sit on his lap. One afternoon, he asked Mom if I could spend the night at his house. Although I didn't want to go, I think Mom felt obligated because of the money he gave us. During that outing, this man sexually molested me.

Of course, he told me to keep it a secret, but shame showed up weeks later when Mom sensed something was off with me. As I shared the details, I was grateful Mom believed me. Instead of contacting the police, she took a friend with her to meet with the man and insisted he was never to come near me again or she would press charges. Thankfully, he never did. However, his shadow still lingered over me, leaving me guarded, paranoid and out of sorts. Sexual abuse is a silent killer, distorting perceptions and trust. Inside, it never felt resolved. Years later, after reading his obituary, I could finally breathe again.

Life at school wasn't much better. Growing up in Detroit meant gangs, break-ins, fist fights, and drug busts. It was common to be beaten, bullied, and teased. It didn't help that I was overweight with buck teeth. Due to busing, houses went up for sale, quickly changing the racial demographics and culture. At school, white girls with long hair dared not go into bathrooms for fear someone would be waiting with scissors, ready to cut off their hair. Personally, I was beaten up twice and had a knife pulled on me. A girl was shot in our school cafeteria. These experiences taught me street smarts and how to remain as invisible as possible. No respite for me.

God did bring sanctuary, but not in the way I expected. An elderly couple who lived down the street adopted two girls. One of the girls befriended me. Living most of her life as a foster child, she found clever ways to do what she wanted in opposition to her parents, including sneaking around with boys. Her family attended a strict Baptist church, where she got excited about the cute guys in the youth group. One Wednesday, she passionately begged me to come because she wanted to teach me how to flirt. Frankly, I wasn't interested, but something deep inside me said I *must* go. So, on that brisk, fall evening, sitting on a swing set, the youth pastor presented the gospel to me, and instead of meeting boys, I met Jesus.

Simultaneously, in the isolation of my room, I discovered another friend—music. The lyrics and melodies of the songs seemed to resonate in the deepest corners of my soul. Music understood me and talent set me apart. Talent provided a new trajectory which included college scholarships, higher social status, and, eventually, a livelihood. Music validated me, and talent celebrated me.

Yet talent didn't come without its price. I spent hours isolated in practice rooms discovering the intense competition in the classical music field. Did I have success? Yes, but not without my share of rejections. My relationship with music inevitably left me unsatisfied. This dissatisfaction became the start of self-awareness about my validation and affirmation deficit. When the big gigs I hoped to get didn't happen, I found myself with deep spiritual questions about God. Did the God I met on that crisp fall night want to keep me from my dreams? Did He even notice me?

After getting married and having two daughters, juggling family and an unstable music career left me with an intense, regimented schedule. With so many responsibilities, any underlying need for validation or affirmation got tucked away. I was an adult now. It was all about the kids. Before I knew it, ten years had gone by, and I found myself enmeshed in a deeply troubled marriage. In an attempt to salvage the relationship, we moved to a small town with limited opportunities. Unnoticed in my career, unseen by my husband, and unvalidated by my church, my heart became an empty cistern looking to be filled.

To combat those feelings, I obsessed over my talents. After all, I was just an ordinary looking girl but at least I could play music! I quickly morphed in being a 'project girl', diving into any type of creative project I could find. While others saw me as defensive and domineering, projects made me feel alive. That is, until the anger, bitterness and envy surfaced. That's when I began to ask myself and God—"What is wrong with me?"

As I became more aware of my deficit, I began to recognize deficits in others. Since nothing seemed to satisfy, I turned to God for answers. As I sought Him out, He took notice of the little girl who needed protection, the teenager resting on her talents, and the adult woman trying to survive. He saw my heart bleeding during my divorce. He showed me how the mercy of the cross ultimately satisfies. The transformation in my thinking, in my attitude, amazes me to this day. This transformation led to others experiencing me differently and describing me as having a 'mysterious' confidence. But there is no mystery. Confidence comes as transformation stories are revealed, allowing us to get a firm grasp on mercy.

My dear readers, I share my story with you, because I want you to know that I'm right there with you. I know what it's like to feel unacknowledged. I know what it's like to feel invisible. I suspect you too, have a story that may have drawn you to this book. Maybe you have struggled when others noticed your attractive friend, but not you. Perhaps you grew up fatherless, were sexually abused, or struggled for others to notice your talents. Or perhaps you're reading this book because you want to be sure your children are acknowledged and celebrated.

I know our experiences won't be the same, or the messages we receive may be different, but I'm confident of this: the enemy's agenda is the same. He wants to distract you by focusing on your feeling of unworthiness as if it defines you. He wants you to waste time on identity pursuits which don't satisfy. Mostly, he doesn't want you to be confident, because then you won't feel worthy enough to paint your masterpiece which brings glory to the Master.

Are you aware of what gives you confidence? Do you look to others to satisfy your feelings of unworthiness? The first step of self-awareness is to admit the need. Unfortunately, as Christians, we are reluctant to admit our need for affirmation because it appears self-serving. Please be reassured. This book doesn't support the lust for attention. Instead, it encourages us to live in the uncomfortableness of feeling unworthy, knowing that the cross says it all. By learning to live with these feelings of unworthiness, we rest in knowing His death sends us a more satisfying message: you're worth it!

Consider this an invitation to join me on this journey to get a firm grasp. As you transform, grasp a life where it's okay to admit your need without feeling selfish. Grasp a life where you understand how to receive and give acknowledgment and celebrate others. Get ready. Your masterpiece awaits!

Because of mercy,

Susan
HOEKSTRA

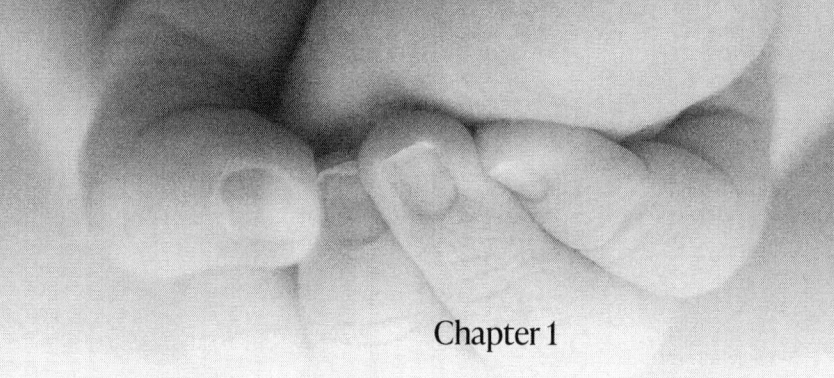

Chapter 1

THE HANDSHAKE

*Open my eyes, that I may behold wondrous
things out of your law.*
—**Psalm 119:18**

*So they said to him,
'Then how were your eyes opened?'*
—**John 9:10**

Running late on a Sunday morning, my family and I arrived at a new church where a gentleman greeted us at the front door. "Welcome," he said, with a grin a mile wide and a warm, generous spirit. With his exceptionally firm handshake still lingering on my fingers, we entered the packed church, struggling to find seats. As we stumbled into the darkened sanctuary, the lights suddenly went up as the preacher instructed us to turn around and shake hands with someone beside us.

Okay, folks, I just have to say it. Awkward. Aside from the obvious germ issues, this tradition just feels uncomfortable to me. We don't do this at a concert or sporting event, so why at church?

Letting out a big sigh, and not wanting to appear rude, I reluctantly engaged. Suddenly, as if a zoom lens appeared, I took notice of how others were responding. Yes! They were just as uncomfortable as I! You could see it in how they approached the handshake.

First, there was the limp handshake, which seemed to say, "I don't know how to do this." Then the pullback, which whispers, "Do I have to?" The clam handshake reaches out to you but leaves you wanting to wipe off the sweat. Next comes the high-five and fist bump, making you feel like a dude hanging out with your bros. Then there's the cower, the handshake which apologizes. Lastly, we can't forget the handshake of all handshakes. You know. The one with so much enthusiasm you think your hand is going to fall off!

What was this all about? Should I care? Why did some have a firm handshake while others didn't? Why are some people more confident than others?

As my curiosity bubbled to the surface, in usual fashion, I did some research. I discovered the Quakers popularized the tradition of shaking hands in the church. The intention behind the handshake was to make a statement that we are all equal under God.

Handshakes carry other meanings. A firm handshake reflects confidence. We've heard stories of dads teaching their sons how to 'properly' shake hands. After all, handshakes seal job interviews, sales agreements, and business deals.

My observations didn't stop there. I became increasingly aware of different levels of confidence in individuals, including myself. I recalled moments of insecurity and self-doubt. I took notice of two-year-old temper tantrums, women vying for affection, and men in mid-life crisis. This progression led me to see the connection. It starts with a handshake.

The handshake reveals our confidence level. To feel confident, we need to feel good about ourselves. To feel good about ourselves, we need to be noticed. To feel noticed, we need to be validated and affirmed.

VALIDATION and AFFIRMATION defined

Since we have a primal need to feel good about ourselves, the way we receive validation and affirmation may result in misconceptions.

For this book's purposes, we are defining validation as "*acknowledgment* of someone's essence, perspective, or experience."

Validation is crucial, and God's establishment of free will supports validation as a fundamental human right. We all have a right to our space, our perspective, and the opportunity for self-expression of our experiences. It's a basic human need to have someone acknowledge us.

Affirmation is slightly different. For this book's purposes, affirmation is "the *approval* of someone's essence, perspective, or experience."

Affirmation essentially is agreeing with someone. These days, we often crave approval because we haven't been acknowledged. It's as if our culture says you only love me if you agree.

One of the challenges of admitting our need for validation and affirmation is that it does make us dependent on others. Perhaps we don't feel alive unless someone else notices us. Essentially, God created us to be in community and have our initial needs met within a community context. The first community that existed is the Trinity—God the Father, God the Son, and God the Holy Spirit. God always existed as a triune community. Each validates and affirms the other.

God further established communities like nations, marriage, and family, who supply many of our validation and affirmation needs. Think back to when your parents became enchanted with your first smile or you got an "atta boy" from your coach. Validation acknowledged your right to have space in the world and get past your self-consciousness. Affirmation gave you the confidence to try new things. Indeed, it's okay to admit that God created us to be validated (acknowledged) and affirmed (approved).

The deficit

However, sometimes our primary community did not adequately meet our need, resulting in a deficit. The evidence for this deficit is compelling. Today, individuals and groups do not feel heard, seen, and are easily offended. The onset of micro-aggressions and movements like #MeToo is telling. And though social media encourages self-expression, it entices us to want more. Selfies, websites, podcasts, blogs, and videos showcase the need. We take vigil on posts and receive satisfaction by how many likes or positive comments we get. If we're honest, these affirming words linger on our hearts for days.

The opposite may be true. Maybe a negative post takes us into a dark place. Are we cultivating a need to be more than just validated or affirmed? Could we be aching to be a celebrity?

Mark Snoeberger from Detroit Baptist Theological Seminary talks about the celebrity concept when he states: "Instead, these problems are symptomatic of a more serious one: the problem of celebrity. The English word *celebrity* derives from the Latin word *celebrer,* "to frequent" and more remotely from the Latin *celer,* "to hasten." The desire for celebrity is, at its heart, the desire of a person to be "frequented"—to turn heads and command the notice of others. To become a celebrity is to succeed in being noticed regularly."

We may not have a need to be a celebrity, but validation and affirmation are important to our development. We all need a compliment or two to keep us going. However, if we crave or seek it out obsessively, it may be something God wants to heal. Where are you on that spectrum? Do you desire for someone's approval or are you okay with being validated? How much do you crave words of affirmation? How does it correspond with your deficit?

The author

Like any need, if we're not careful, a desire for affirmation can turn to lust. Just like hunger can become gluttony, sex can escalate to adultery, and leadership interest can turn to power lust, the need to be noticed can lead to approbation lust. Approbation lust is an untamed desire to be seen and approved. The Scriptures reveal to us the originator of this lust pattern.

Radiating light and glory, covered with gold and shimmering jewels, the author of needing excessive attention is Lucifer. Lucifer was one of heaven's top three angels. He was beautiful, immensely talented in music, academics, and administration and responsible for worship as the lead musician. Ezekiel 28:12-14 explains him this way:*"You were the signet of perfection, full of wisdom and perfect in beauty. You were in Eden, the garden of God; every precious stone was your covering, sardius, topaz, and diamond, beryl, onyx, and jasper, sapphire, emerald, and carbuncle; and crafted in gold were your settings and your engravings. On the day that you were created, they were prepared. You were an anointed guardian cherub. I placed you; you were on the holy mountain of God; in the midst of the stones of fire you walked."*

With that kind of description, I'm sure all of us would have noticed Lucifer. He was a celebrity! As the angel with stunning looks and incredible talent, he was not unlike our stars today. Yet, he took it too far. Leading angels to worship God, Lucifer began to resent the attention given to God. He thought he was just as special as God, so why wasn't anyone taking notice of him?

Ezekiel 28:17 describes Satan's mindset: *"Your heart was proud because of your beauty; you corrupted your wisdom for the sake of your splendor. I cast you to the ground; I exposed you before kings, to feast their eyes on you."*

Isaiah 14:13 says, *"You said in your heart, 'I will ascend to heaven; above the stars of God, I will set my throne on high; I will sit on the mount of assembly in the far reaches of the north.'"*

Lucifer's untamed desire left him without self-awareness. He didn't see himself for who he was. It wasn't enough for Lucifer to be in the presence of God and be His chief of staff. He wanted more. He felt unnoticed. He didn't receive acknowledgment nor the affirmation he desired. Like a snowball effect, those feelings fueled insecurity. Insecurity leads to approbation lust. Approbation lust, or any other kind of lust, never satisfies. Friends, if this is the heart of Satan, wouldn't it be reasonable to think he would want to entice us in the same way?

Comparing ourselves to others promotes jealousy and envy. Focusing on our insecurities or seeking unnecessary attention diminishes our effectiveness for God. Although insecurity can often come across as pride, at its root, it is the feeling of inadequacy. Jeremy Pierre, Associate Professor of Biblical Counseling at Southern Baptist Theological Seminary, further explains insecurity this way in his article in *The Gospel Coalition*: "God disapproves of our insecurity because it is an offense to His Son's worthiness. Insecurity is confidence in the flesh. Insecurity gums up our ability to do what God made us to do: love him and others. How many times have you been in a situation where you should have offered care to someone or approached God privately in prayer, but your mind is slogging through another round of how awkward you look in your pants that morning or how much smarter than you the person is to whom you're talking? Being self-conscious is being conscious of self. We do not love others when we are obsessing with ourselves; we are not in humility. Our dissatisfaction with self is often nothing more than our dissatisfaction with God. Insecurity is not sinful because it is an insult to our value (though it is), but because it is an insult to God's wisdom."

Our model

Thankfully, we have an opposite model in Jesus. Even though He was human and God simultaneously, He was confident in who He was and in His Father's mission. We don't see Jesus being self-conscious, insecure or excessively needing affirmation anywhere. John 6 gives us a gentle reminder. After feeding over 5,000 people, healing the sick, and performing miracles, Jesus became somewhat of a celebrity. With His fame at its peak, the crowds were ready to crown Him King, and the disciples saw this as a remarkable marketing opportunity. If He was King, couldn't He potentially glorify God even more through His celebrity status? But that's not how Jesus responded in John 6:15: *"Perceiving then that they were about to come and take him by force to make him king, Jesus withdrew again to the mountain by himself."* In John 8:50, He said, *"Yet I do not seek my own glory; there is One who seeks it, and he is the judge."*

Jesus had three years to do ministry. Being self-conscious or seeking fame before it was time would only distract Him. Instead, His focus was on the presence of God, the Father, and the mission.

Just as he tried to distract Jesus regarding His mission, Satan tries to keep us distracted. Insecurities prevent us from moving forward. Why is it that we have trouble accepting that someone else could be more…than us? Friends, we can't all be Olympic athletes or rocket scientists. Awareness and acknowledgement of our limitations, mistakes, and sins, help us stop striving.

However, like Lucifer, we don't like to feel less than, and will try anything to keep from feeling insecure. We dislike the discomfort of something being wrong with us. Take a look at any self-help aisle at the local bookstore, and you will see the need. Without even knowing it, we try to compensate by taking on another's persona, or become actors filling a role. A way we try to fill that hole is to seek out excessive affirmation while simultaneously denying our uniqueness.

The temptation

Since this is part of our enemy's deepest character flaw, he continues to tempt us. He even tempted Jesus! Let's see how Satan tempted Jesus in Matthew 4:1-6:

> *Then Jesus was led up by the Spirit into the wilderness to be tempted by the devil. And after fasting forty days and forty nights, he was hungry. And the tempter came and said to him, "If you are the Son of God, command these stones to become loaves of bread." But he answered—"It is written, "Man shall not live by bread alone but by every word that comes from the mouth of God." Then the devil took him to the holy city and set him on the pinnacle of the temple and said to him, "If you are the Son of God, throw yourself down, for it is written "He will command his angels concerning you,' and on their hands they will bear you up, lest you strike your foot against a stone."*

Take notice of the *if you are* statements. This implies a direct attack on Jesus' identity. Maybe Satan assumed Jesus was just as insecure as he was and needed to be validated and affirmed. Perhaps Satan couldn't see past his own pride. Remember, his goal is to get Jesus off mission. By doing that, God's plan of salvation wouldn't be fulfilled.

Friends, I don't believe Jesus spent time in the self-help aisle searching for His identity. Jesus understood who He was. He knew

He was God and human at the same time. Because He had a firm grasp on who He was, and His mission, He didn't feel insecure, nor have a need to explain Himself. He didn't challenge the devil's question or desire worship. He didn't get defensive nor feel offended. Instead, He used scripture as His 'default.' See how He confidently replies in Matthew 4:7; *Jesus said to him: "Again, it is written, You shall not put the Lord your God to the test. It is written: Man shall not live on bread alone, but on every word that comes from the mouth of God."*

He knew He was God and man at the same time. I wonder if He sealed the deal with a firm handshake.

Our response

As humans, let's face it, we're inconsistent. We vacillate daily between feelings of confidence and insecurity. I especially notice this about myself when I'm around someone who has an 'aura' of confidence. At first I feel intimidated, but secretly, I wonder. What makes them feel so self-assured? Are they covering up their insecurities? Do they have a firm grasp on something I don't understand?

Vacillations happen when we care too much about what others think. Perhaps no one was there to affirm or validate us as we grew up, creating a deficit. One way to compensate is to behave in an overly self-confident or even cocky manner. Or sometimes we become self-effacing by demonstrating negative self-talk. Some of us respond by ignoring the need by becoming invulnerable. Usually, we're trying to protect ourselves or cover up our hurts.

I didn't become cocky or self-effacing but by becoming an invulnerable person, I would dominate a room. This was my attempt to avoid potential hurts. When I felt like a misfit in social settings, I became a chameleon, adapting to others values as my own. This led me to be a classic enabler. Outwardly, I seemed empathetic, yet inwardly, I had an overwhelming feeling that others had a handle on things, but somehow, I didn't. I couldn't be vulnerable and let them know what I was really feeling.

After years of living this way, I eventually conceded. I drew the conclusion many people do: something must be wrong with me. Without knowing who I was or who I wanted to be, I felt lost. Research convinced me that somewhere out there was an answer. So, I started taking personality assessments and reading self-help books. Although the evaluations and workbooks gave me some clarity, they were only a temporary fix. Part of the reason they didn't satisfy was they led me to comparison. Once comparison started, I was either flying high on confidence or flying low with insecurity. In my quest to get more information, I researched, read, and strived. All of these are signs of self-help. After all, understanding must be the spiritual process of transformation I read about, right?

Kenneth Boa, President of Reflections Ministry and Trinity House Publishing, talks about the Christian life being a process, not a destination in his book *Conformed to His Image*. He explained: "In our society, we increasingly tend to be human doings rather than human beings. The world tells us that what we achieve and accomplish determines who we are, but the Scriptures teach that who we are in Christ should be the basis for what we do. The dynamics of growth are inside-out rather than outside-in. Process spirituality is concerned with faithfulness during the ongoing journey rather than living from one product to the next. It also focuses on what it means to abide in Christ and to practice His presence."

Yes, transformation is a process. Transformation begins when we become aware of our humanity, and ultimately say, "I surrender." But, more than that, if we can truly see and validate ourselves as we are—both good and bad—we can let go of our feelings about ourselves and radiate His presence.

Chapter 1 – The Handshake

How could a simple handshake mean so much?

After the church service ended, we headed towards the door. In the corner, I saw the man who initially greeted us. Hoping to miss him and any awkwardness, I approached the door, but before I knew it, there he was. With a grin a mile wide, he couldn't help himself. And so, I shook his clammy hand—this time, with confidence.

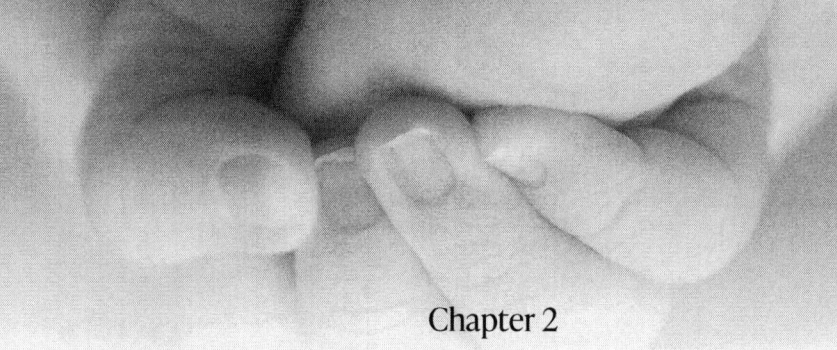

Chapter 2

Give and Take

――――――――― " ―――――――――

*The greatness of a man's power is
the measure of his surrender.*
—**William Booth**

*"For whoever would save his life will lose it,
but whoever loses his life for my sake
and the gospel's will save it."*
—**Mark 8:35**

As I was developing a classical music career, I recall preparing for an audition into a prestigious music college for my master's degree. To reach a high level of excellence in the performing arts requires dedication and discipline. I lived in the practice room. However, I wanted to go to this college so much it became an unhealthy obsession. I practiced for hours on end, had every musician I knew listen to my audition, and exhausted my friends with my "what if" scenarios. I honestly believed getting into this particular college was going to determine my entire destiny!

Maybe you guessed what came next. I wasn't accepted. To this day, I don't know the reason why, although I drew all kinds of conclusions. This rejection forced me to face my deepest fear—the root of it all—not being good enough. The next few weeks were spent in tears, overwrought with questions and sinking into a dark hole. I had done the work yet didn't get the result. Was it my lack of talent? Could it be my socio-economic background? Did this mean I should stop trying to be a professional musician?

Friends and family offered platitudes like "where God closes a door, He opens a window," or "They don't know what they are missing." I knew they were well intentioned, but honestly, these cliches made me want to scream! Instead of acknowledging my experience, I felt like they were trying to talk me out of what I was feeling so I would move on. Without validation, my rejection turned into paranoia and hypersensitivity.

Hypervigilance

Of course, no one likes to be rejected. The word *rejection* comes from a Latin word which means to be thrown back. Sometimes rejection causes us to retreat. Other times, we start blaming others for our failures. Either way, we're thrown off course.

Being accepted into a prestigious college doesn't have to be the goal; a variety of events can thwart dreams. Maybe you, like me, respond by protecting yourself. When no one seemed to understand, my response was to become obsessed with every detail around me. Others might say I had a strong need to control or wanted to be the alpha in the room. I wasn't aware then, but this kind of high alert is known as hypervigilance—an enhanced state of sensory sensitivity.

Hypervigilance can show up in a variety of ways, but mostly as a strong need to establish the emotional climate in the room. What I was denying was my deepest need: approval. I refused to admit my need, because then I was giving someone else way too much power in my life. Instead, I buried it inside.

One way I buried it was to convince myself it's someone or something else besides me or the way I responded. In my pride, I convinced myself that setting a goal and striving for perfection is something we all should be doing. Never mind that I would push my goals onto others and look down on them if they didn't comply. As I became keenly aware of each action or word, I was quick to attack and started judging others for their lack of vigilance. As I tried to protect myself from another rejection, others only experienced my intensity. Thank God this was just a season in my life. Otherwise, I'd be a very lonely girl.

Hypervigilance is often rooted on something real—a rejection or traumatic event with severe, understandable consequences. Maybe you were sexually abused as a child. Due to that experience, when you became a mother, you found yourself adamant your children will not spend the night at anyone's house. This type of protection is reasonable, and wise. However, if you take it too far, it may become fear-based hypervigilance.

Give it

Psychology offers us many solutions to hypervigilance. Cognitive behavioral therapy, medications, and EMDR (Eye Movement Desensitization and Reprocessing) are all ways to get relief if it is negatively affecting your day-to-day life. Maybe God is making you aware of your hypervigilance now. Have faith, dear friends. God offers a solution too. But it requires us to give in and give it. It's called surrender.

God calls us to rest. God calls us to peace. When we're hypervigilant, we're not at peace. Our fears blind us to our lusts or fuel us to work excessively hard to impress others. We may feel justified because we're good at what we're doing, or we conclude no one else can do it as well as we can. As for me, I wasn't even aware I was hypervigilant and certainly didn't think I was domineering. I thought I was actually surrendering. After all, I had good intentions. I gave 'it' to God—but then I took it back. I call it the give and take.

Doing the give and take is part of being human. Years ago, I remember doing this at a weekend youth group retreat in upper Michigan. One evening at a bonfire, our youth pastor talked about surrender. At the end of his talk, he asked us to do something. As pieces of paper and pens were passed around, he instructed us to write down someone or something we were struggling to surrender to God. After praying and writing it down, we put our papers in the fire, watching as they evaporated into the night sky. This was to symbolize us giving "it" to God. I'm not sure what others wrote, but as a teenager, my something was someone—a guy I liked. As my paper went up in smoke, I felt the surrender. And I truly meant it.

Yet, weeks later, I took it back.

Active or passive

Do you ever wonder what it would be like to completely surrender…to sing "I Surrender All" and truly give it *all* to Jesus? Gary Thomas, in his book *Seeking the Face of God*, makes this statement: "Christian health is not defined by how happy we are, how prosperous or healthy we are, or even by how many people we have led to the Lord in the past year. Christian health is ultimately defined by how sincerely we wave our flag of surrender."

Aside from the give and take, what does surrender really look like? Sometimes passive and sometimes active.

Chapter 2 – Give and Take

Passive surrender is what we think of when we "raise the white flag." It's that give up moment when we feel cornered and cannot hide. Passive surrender happens when we realize there is no other choice. Powerless, we have no choice but to surrender.

When we 'actively' surrender, we make a deliberate choice. We choose to relinquish control. We make a decision that God ultimately decides what is best for us. We may start by surrendering idols or hypervigilance. Maybe we surrender our striving.

As the lines between active and passive surrender are blurred, we can't position ourselves to transform without surrender. Surrender is an act of the will. You cannot go through the journey of this book without a 'Come to Jesus' moment where you give in and let God do what He is going to do. We don't surrender for surrender's sake. God has a purpose to our surrender—to set us apart.

Allow me to explain the process of transformation with an analogy from the silversmith. During the cleansing process for removing oxidation from silver, a silversmith heats silver in a fire; and as it melts, scum rises to the surface. This scum is known as dross. The silversmith skims off the dross only to heat the silver again, this time at a higher temperature, allowing more dross to rise to the surface. With impurities removed once more, the silversmith repeats the process over and over until he can see his likeness reflected in the silver.

Friends, God is our silversmith. He wants those who observe us to see His reflection. We can best reflect Him when we allow the dross in our life to surface for purification. Don't be alarmed. God sees impurities rising to the surface as cleansing and understands our give and take. That's why He skims off our surrender, and repeats the process over and over. By allowing the dross to rise, we are cleansed. Once cleansed, we are equipped to focus on the mission because we reflect our Master.

It all begins with surrender.

Proverbs 25:4 explains: *"Take away the dross from the silver; and the smith has material for a vessel."* 2 Timothy 2:21 tells us: *"Therefore, if anyone cleanses himself from what is dishonorable, he will be a vessel for honorable use, set apart as holy, useful to the master of the house, ready for every good work."*

Based on our dross, what we surrender will be unique to us. Perhaps our dross includes the way we respond to life by retreating, accusing, or criticizing others to make ourselves feel better. Maybe we try to imitate others to avoid our feelings of inadequacy. Perhaps we strive by taking personality profiles to help us accept our dross. The dross in our life isn't just the experiences we've had, the sin that we've committed, but includes the sins others committed against us and the way we've responded to them.

Allowing the dross to rise and altering our responses are part of the sanctification process. The sanctification process begins with acknowledgment of our dross. The first step is when the Holy Spirit draws us to salvation. At this stage, we acknowledge our sin and need for a Savior. John 6:44 tells us, *"No one can come to me unless the Father who sent me draws them…"* and Acts 2:21 states, *"And it shall come to pass that everyone who calls on the name of the Lord shall be saved."*

If you are not a child of God, I pray that you will accept His salvation gift. Acknowledge your failure to meet His standards, accept His punishment in the form of Jesus Christ (who paid the penalty for your sin), and surrender your life to Him. He will hear your voice and welcome you with open arms into the family of God. I guarantee, you will be celebrated!

If you've done that, perhaps it's time to take another layer off. Write on a piece of paper what you need to surrender next. Maybe it's your desperate longing for validation. Maybe it's the secret wish you have to be a star or the fact that your parents weren't there for you. The more we surrender, the less we look like us, and the more we look like Jesus. The more we surrender to the Spirit, the more fruit we produce.

Galatians 5:22-23 describes this fruit in vivid detail: *"But the fruit of the Spirit is love, joy, peace, patience, kindness, goodness, faithfulness, gentleness, self-control; against such things there is no law."*

We cannot produce these fruits authentically without the power of the Holy Spirit in our lives. Surrendering our will is how we are sanctified, but it's important to be realistic about ourselves. It's more of a give and take. At first, we will give God control of certain areas of our life but take others for ourselves. As time goes on, we'll give over more, and God will reveal to us the next thing to surrender. It may be as simple as finding a parking spot or as complex as surrendering our marriage. Romans 6:13 states:*"Do not present your members to sin as instruments for unrighteousness but present yourselves to God as those who have been brought from death to life, and your members to God as instruments for righteousness.*

Idols

We can't talk about surrender without talking about idols. God takes idolatry seriously. The first two of the Ten Commandments talk about this in detail.

Exodus 20:3-6 tells us, *"You shall have no other gods before me. You shall not make for yourself a carved image, or any likeness of anything that is in heaven above, or that is in the earth beneath, or that is in the water under the earth. You shall not bow down to them or serve them, for I the Lord your God am a jealous God, visiting the iniquity of the fathers on the children to the third and the fourth generation of those who hate me, but showing steadfast love to thousands of those who love me and keep my commandments."*

Perhaps our vision of idolatry looks more like worshipping statues as in the Old Testament. Executive Pastor Jack Magruder of Trinity Church, in a recent episode of "The Notice" podcast, gave a great definition of idols: "An idol is anything, any person, or any attitude where you are seeking something that rightfully comes from God."

What are you seeking? Do you need to be accepted into a prestigious music college? If you haven't recognized or taken the time to process the dross in your life through surrender, I invite you to reconsider. As the dross rises, you will be a purified vessel, ready to shine for God.

Giving In

As you proceed, be sure your expectations are realistic. Go ahead and accept the give and take of your humanity. Just know that if you take it back, God will repeat the process. Since He is a God of healing, I assure you, He does this for your own good. He doesn't want you to live in hypervigilance or strife. He wants you to be at rest. Eventually, He wants to replace the give and take with giving in. Giving in is living connected to Him moment by moment, surrendering everything, including that parking spot.

As you give in, you'll take notice. You will start to see the ways God is there for you. You'll begin to notice little things each day that remind you of His presence and how He validates and affirms you in ways you never thought possible. If you're protecting yourself, stop. Stop and take time to surrender. In order to accomplish this, God may ask you to be still.

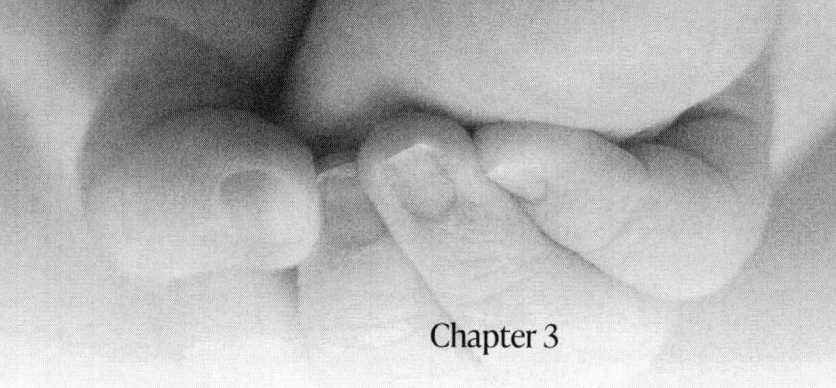

Chapter 3

Be Still

―――――― " ――――――

Be still and know that I am God.
—**Psalm 46:10**

The Lord will fight for you; you only need to be still.
—**Exodus 14:4**

Feeling the fresh air as I opened the windows, my heart couldn't help but smile. It was a beautiful Saturday morning, and the sun was a welcome sight. After three straight days of rain, clouds, work, and quarantine, I was excited to get outside and take a walk. The neighborhood welcomed my mood. I noticed tulips and daffodils in full bloom, plants emerging, and leaves budding on the trees. Spring had finally come.

As I continued my stroll, I noticed all the things people were doing despite COVID 19 like working in the yard, walking dogs, and mowing lawns. One neighbor put a smile on my face as I spotted her huge outdoor tent complete with lounge chairs and a tv in her backyard. But perhaps what excited me most was how incredibly friendly everyone was. It was as if they were genuinely glad to see me, even though we had never met.

After my sixth or seventh conversation with neighbors I hadn't met before, I headed home. But it was not without considering just what made everyone so friendly. Certainly, sunshine changes our mood. I also recalled that I hadn't seen anyone else in person, except for my husband, for three days. The funny thing is, when I'm home more and have fewer people to talk to, I find myself noticing more. I notice leaves, the blowing wind, people sitting on their porches, and the squirrel running across the street. Sometimes, despite the hectic pace of life, it seems the only way to take notice is to slow down.

Too busy to notice

Think about the last time you asked someone how they were doing. They probably replied they were "busy" rather than returning the customary response of "fine." Caught up in the fast pace of life and juggling many demands, busy seems to be our new badge of honor. Although we know twenty-four hours is still twenty-four hours, we make the mistake of trying to accomplish more within that time frame. What transpires? We become too busy to notice and struggle to be present. Instead, anxiety, stress, and impatience cripple us.

Others of us enjoy being busy. I get it. On some level, busy feeds us, makes us feel important, and keeps us from being bored. Perhaps it started when our parents encouraged us that our hard work would pay off by filling up our calendars. Perhaps we stay busy to avoid something. Even overscheduling can be an unconscious excuse to avoid unpleasant people or issues in life.

God made us to be productive, and He wants us to serve Him by serving others. Yet, He also made us for relationship and worship. We may fail to acknowledge others because we can't hear the needs of others without being present. And we can't be present without being still. Being still allows us to sense the give and take of surrender. Surrender encourages us to release control. Releasing control will enable us to allow the dross to rise so we can be cleansed.

In order to accomplish this, we have to plan time to be still. It's more than being still; it's a mindset to prioritize processing time. Christian mindfulness helps us notice God, the relationships in our life, and our inner world of thoughts and feelings. This spiritual discipline is an art.

To experience this art, the best place to start is first and foremost with God Himself. Nothing in our lives is too small or insignificant for Him to notice. He noticed the Hebrews groaning under Egyptian bondage. He knows the number of hairs on our head, and intimately notices our pains, joys and dross. Psalms 56:8 (NLT) tells us, *"You keep track of all my sorrows. You have collected all my tears in your bottle. You have recorded each one in your book."*

If you're anything like me, you don't really know how to be still. It's downright uncomfortable. Silence makes me feel anxious, tempting my flesh to do something, anything, to break the silence. Even though I crave silence, when I'm around others, it's challenging for me not to talk. I'm the first to speak, or the first to scurry with activity to fill up empty spaces. Here's the best part. When I don't pause, I jump into problem-solving mode, attempting to fix a problem that isn't mine to fix. Impatient, I fail to live the Exodus 14:4 life: *"The Lord will fight for you, you need only to be still."*

The struggle to be present is real for all of us. As mentioned in the previous chapter, we give our burdens to God, then take them back. His desire is for us to set everything else aside to make room for Him. Sometimes all it takes is a sigh.

The Spiritual Sigh

To make room for what God has for us, it's good to realize that being still is more than stopping activity or taking a vacation. Being still is a mindset. As we are still, we develop the spiritual skill of rest. We find ourselves less likely to strive or attempt to prove ourselves to anyone, whether intentionally or subconsciously. Physically, emotionally, mentally, and spiritually, we rest. Getting quiet allows us to hear His voice. But how do we cultivate that sense of stillness in the middle of it all?

If you find yourself feeling disconnected with God, one option may be to go on a retreat. Retreats are an excellent opportunity to dig deeper and get a break from daily routines. Not all of us can do that, so how can we be still without going away? For me, one way I am still with God is through His creation. I purposely plan times to connect with God through a walk in the woods, hearing waves crash, or spending time outdoors. I don't need an entire weekend to do this. Even a short walk can calm me.

When you live in northern Michigan, it's a good idea to love the outdoors, and to love snow. It snows a lot! One of the activities I enjoy is cross-country skiing. Deep in the woods in my happy place. I enjoy the immaculately groomed trails and stunning silence. I can hear the wind howl and the sounds of a nearby creek. If I listen carefully, it is so quiet, that I can actually hear the snow fall. It's pure magic.

Nature provides me just the right white noise to relax me and assist me in the artistic process. On one particular ski excursion, I found myself a little anxious. As all kinds of music I was preparing for concerts poured in and out of my head, I noticed this time, this afternoon, something was different.

Abruptly, as if a switch turned off, the music in my head ceased. A bench was nearby, so I rested, taking in the stillness. As it continued to snow, I let out a huge sigh. Prayers organically flowed as I enveloped myself in the beauty and power of God's creation. As I exhaled my burdens, I inhaled His presence. Then it happened.

The tune and words to my very first song, *Be Still*, appeared as I was sitting on that snowy bench. Experiencing God's presence literally stopped me in my tracks. God invited me to slow down and catch my breath. I'm not sure if it was taking Him in or exhaling my burdens, but I felt at peace and inspired. I felt alive. I felt the strength which comes from being in His presence. And I wanted more.

Cross-country skiing in the north woods is only one way to quiet yourself in God's creation. Maybe you like taking a walk, listening to music, sitting by the beach, or taking a bath. No matter what the activity, are you still? Can you see yourself breathing? If you can see yourself breathing, can you breathe again? Can you feel yourself sigh?

In scripture, being still is synonymous with being in God's presence. Jesus took the time to be alone with God, emulating peace amidst the chaos. He withdrew, mourned, and modeled physical rest.

Luke 6:16 tells us, *"But Jesus often withdrew to lonely places to pray."* After John the Baptist was beheaded, Jesus took time to mourn. He retreated. Matthew 14:13 describes the scene: *"Now when Jesus heard this, he withdrew from there in a boat to a desolate place by himself."*

Jesus also modeled physical rest when He fell asleep in the boat amid a raging storm and appeared unapologetic about getting the rest He needed. Mark 4:37-39 describes the scene: *"And a great windstorm arose, and the waves were breaking into the boat, so that the boat was already filling. But he was in the stern, asleep on the cushion. And they woke him and said to him, "Teacher, do you not care that we are perishing?" And he awoke and rebuked the wind and said to the sea, "Peace! Be still!" And the wind ceased, and there was a great calm."*

Inhale and exhale

Calmness begins when we stop to be still enough to notice who is in the boat with us. Recently, our church implemented a two-minute silence habit. During two minutes of silence, you can pray, breathe, or meditate. Or you can do what I experienced in the woods: The Spiritual Sigh. The Spiritual Sigh includes inhaling and exhaling. Perhaps you can start by putting aside two minutes and utilizing the following steps:

- † Find a quiet place.
- † Take a deep breath and sigh.
- † Exhale your racing thoughts.
- † Inhale one or more of His attributes.

   God is sovereign – the final authority.

   God is omniscient – all-knowing.

   God is omnipresent – everywhere at once.

   God is veracity – the truth.

   God is immutable – He never changes.

   God is justice – He is fair.

   God is eternal – He always existed.

   God is merciful – He doesn't seek to punish.

   God is love – God is love.

   God is righteous – He is 100% pure.

- † Exhale your burdens.
- † Repeat

As you inhale, go ahead and meditate by combining His attributes. For example, we know His justice is loving, His mercy never changes, and His authority is truthful.

Chapter 3 – Be Still

One also can't forget God's amazing grace. His grace is so intricate, it has multiple parts. Saving grace, logistical grace, bountiful grace, and dying grace. His saving grace removes our condemnation. His logistical grace keeps us alive through provision. Bountiful grace is given to us as we mature spiritually, and dying grace transfers us from time into eternity. As God's grace sustains us, His mercy loves us, and His attributes humble us.

As you catch your breath, let go. During the sigh, God will bring to the surface new perspectives, opportunities, and insights. He may even reveal some of your dross. God will use anything to reveal Himself to us. Maybe He will use this book to reveal issues to you, or perhaps He is showing you situations when you have to stop problem-solving for everyone else.

As my dross rose to the surface, God gently invited me to self-examine. For example, in one of my be still moments, He revealed how much problem-solving fed me. By offering my advice, I came across to others as domineering. As I gained self-awareness, I realized solving problems made me feel good about myself, satisfying a deep-seated need for validation and affirmation. Deep down, I counteracted my feelings of inadequacy with pride. As tough as it was to discover these things about myself, God reminded me this self-awareness was a step towards healing. He wanted me to be aware enough to let go. I don't think I would have come to that realization without stillness.

What about you? Do you routinely take time to be still? Can you take two minutes to be silent? Many books and articles teach us how to enter into His presence. Keep in mind that God is omnipresent—everywhere simultaneously—we just need to access Him. Other times, you may sense God's presence more vividly than at other times as I did in the woods. This is called manifestation.

If you know what it's like to feel God's presence, I encourage you to practice the Spiritual Sigh. Be still and dwell on His attributes.

When you remember that God is everywhere simultaneously because He's omnipresent, you will know He's there even if you don't feel His presence. Faith believes in something you can't see. Experiences aren't necessary to affirm His presence.

As you are still, look around...take notice. Perhaps you notice Him in the snow-covered hills, through a baby's smile, or when He shows you the right parking spot. Maybe He's taking notice of you right now. Can you see it? When we notice how He notices, we notice how He acknowledges and celebrates us. That's a lot of noticing!

Waiting

Being still to dwell on God's essence takes time and requires self-control and patience. I promise, the enemy will not want you to wait. He will want you to seek validation or affirmation in other places instead of waiting on God. He will want you to dwell on the dross in your life as if it defines you. He will give you reasons to take care of whatever it is by yourself through hypervigilance.

It takes courage and maturity to rest. If you think it's time to move on, stop. Take a breath, let out the Spiritual Sigh, and repeat until you feel your heartbeat. As your circumstances dim, accept the invitation from Matthew 11:28-30: *"Come to me, all who labor and are heavy laden, and I will give you rest. Take my yoke upon you, and learn from me, for I am gentle and lowly in heart, and you will find rest for your souls. For my yoke is easy, and my burden is light."*

As you become more aware of your need for validation and affirmation, recognize your tendency to give and take, then go head, and be still. As you read the following chapters, they may reveal something you need to process. As you inhale His presence and let the dross rise to the surface, you will receive a new set of eyes. You'll notice He is *for* you, not against you. You'll notice you are His shining star.

Chapter 3 – Be Still

Some chapters include songs to complement the topics. You are invited to go to my website and listen to BE STILL.

For reflection purposes, you will also see a link to a "Soaking Session" which includes songs I've written and instrumental music I played on the clarinet, infused with scripture and quotes from the book. I invite you to sit down, relax, and share it with others. May if offer you a great way to be still.

LISTEN TO: Be Still

susanhoekstra.com/songs

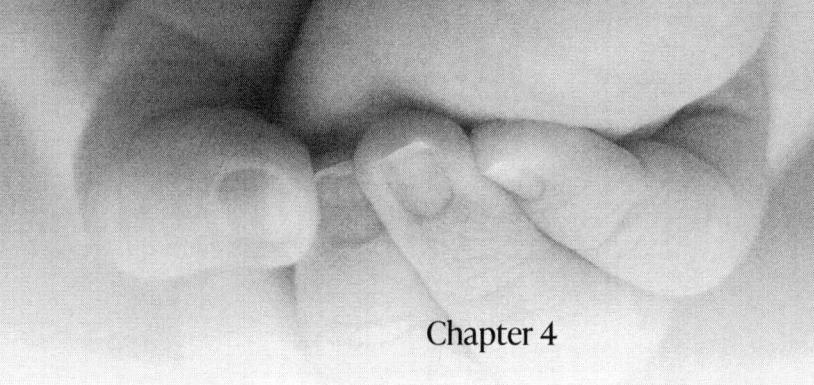

Chapter 4

A STAR IS BORN

———————————— " ————————————

*The heavens declare the glory of God; and the sky
above proclaims His handiwork.*
—**Psalm 19:1**

God loves each of us as if there were only one of us.
—**Augustine**

*There are heavenly bodies and earthly bodies,
but the glory of the heavenly is of one kind, and
the glory of the earthly is of another. There is
one glory of the sun, and another glory of
the moon, and another glory of the stars;
for star differs from star in glory.*
—**1 Corinthians 15:40-41**

There is nothing like looking into the northern Michigan sky on a clear summer night. As you take in the fresh, crisp air, you can't help but notice the multitude of stars against the dark canvas sky. Astrologers tell us there are so many stars we can't see them all.

How bright a star becomes is determined by how big it is or how close to the earth it is. Some shine brighter than others, and some hide.

Stars have been used to send messages from God on high. The Star of Bethlehem was one such beautiful invitation. So, naturally, when we see a star, we want to draw near and connect to a world bigger than us. Fascinated by their brilliance, we may even desire to be stars. Some of us want to be shiny ones.

I vividly remember the very first-time stars were pointed out to me. I felt significant and small at the same time. I also remember the first-time I received a gold star on my school paper. That star meant I did well. I loved the feeling of being noticed for doing something good. It was more than acknowledgement. I loved the approval. I loved being affirmed.

Our need

The desire to get a star on our paper or be a star can motivate us towards greater heights. Artists, musicians, actors, businessmen, and athletes dream of becoming rich and famous. Song lyrics, paintings, literature, and movies highlight stories on the road to stardom. Our parents even encouraged us to work hard to earn rewards. By getting noticed a lot, we may feel like a star. We might even have a fan club.

In the same way, current social media platforms entice stardom. Posts can go viral overnight, providing overnight success. If we're honest, something in us gets stimulated when others like or comment on our posts. Reality shows like *American Idol*, *Survivor*, and *The Bachelor* highlight individuals craving the limelight. To get noticed, we expend energy creating an online image, even if it doesn't correspond with our true selves. Are we searching for our one moment in time?

Chapter 4 – A Star is Born

When we look up in the sky, some stars shine brighter than others, some are larger than others, some shine in a bright burst for a short time, and some stay hidden. We don't always know how big or bright our star will become. Perhaps we don't even think of ourselves as stars. Even if we don't desire to be a star, we all occupy space. Divine space. We are part of a galaxy.

As a result, acknowledging our space—something we are—rather than our action—something we've done—is a great step to gaining a firm grasp. Eventually, we will see that no one else can occupy our space, nor can we do anything to earn that space. Just like stars in the galaxy, the minute we take our first breath, we are given our divine space. A star is born.

Have you ever thought of yourself as a star? Does it make you uncomfortable to think of yourself that way? Could our appreciation of ourselves and each other be enhanced by acknowledging someone else's divine right to the space they were given to reflect God?

Acknowledging our stardom isn't meant to make us feel better about ourselves. Validating our divine space isn't the same as affirmation. Acknowledging our divine space is an 'it is what it is' moment. Affirmation is different than acknowledgment. Acknowledgment is about what God provided for us, not something we did.

Affirmation reinforces what we did is good, which we can mistake for being good. When we admit our need for acknowledgement, we aren't promoting self. Instead, we acknowledge something bigger than ourselves—God—who created a divine space in the universe for us. Friends, this distinction is more than just semantics. Being aware of our divine space encourages confidence in God, in ourselves, and others. Desiring untamed approval from others is more about us and what we do than what God did for us. We need to be careful. Searching for excess approval can have damaging effects.

Taken too far

We can't talk about stardom without bringing up extremes, like narcissism. Needing continual approval can have deep roots. In our culture, Narcissistic Personality Disorder (NPD) is a mental health diagnosis. This kind of personality disorder exhibits extreme beliefs and behaviors. According to the Diagnostic and Statistical Manual of Mental Disorders, those with NPD exhibit impairments in identity, self-esteem regulation, and exaggerated self-appraisal. They vacillate between extremes and set goals based on gaining the approval of others. Their standards are high for others but lower for themselves. Lacking empathy, they have trouble with intimacy and display antagonism. They have a mindset of grandiosity and entitlement and show haughty behaviors or attitudes. Self-centered, they firmly hold to the belief that they are better than others.

I know that's quite a list. The sad part is that those with NPD have an extremely fragile center, lacking a sense of their true selves. They have trouble acknowledging their divine space because they don't trust it. Whenever a threat to an idea or image of their false self comes to the surface, they become distraught. Being enamored with the "idea" of who they are or who they believe they should be, turns attention away from the deep hole within—a deep hole that only enlarges if no one takes notice.

Narcissism is often the topic of many discussions these days. Before we begin to label others, we need to recognize a mental health trend is not the same as a professional diagnosis. Labels can be hurtful because they can easily change a person's sense of identity. Being able to google something doesn't make us an expert either. Some extremes may be related to unresolved traumas or a result of sin. Since all of us are sinners, any need untamed can become a lust pattern. We are all close to falling. The only person we need to evaluate is the person staring at us in the mirror each morning.

Chapter 4 – A Star is Born

The intent of this book is to not to diagnosis. Instead, it's about self-awareness. By acknowledging everyone's divine space, a sacred respect for ourselves and others develop. This awareness doesn't fight when the dross rises to the surface, because we understand we are still stars being purified for good works. Only God, you, or a professional can diagnose whether your need is extreme or not.

Identifying the need

If you have a quest to be recognized, even within your own circles or communities, I encourage you to be mindful. To help you better identify your need, you can take the online assessment of your validation or affirmation deficits on my website: susankhoekstra.com. This assessment isn't a diagnosis, but rather a bridge towards self-awareness. Perhaps you can relate to the following examples.

Maybe you are a mom who desires her husband to notice how hard she works around the house raising children. Maybe you're pining for that promotion at work and become distraught when someone else gets it instead. As a creative person, when your creations don't get a response or reach the masses, you feel unnoticed. Maybe you've struggled with how fat you are, believing only the pretty people can shine. Perhaps you are a woman who believes the best way to get noticed is to post seductive images on social media. Maybe you have unusual skills, but not enough to be famous, so you don't feel like you fit in anywhere. Just like the toys in the *Rudolph, the Red-Nosed Reindeer* movie, you may feel like a misfit.

Many musicians and artists who ended up stars felt like a misfit at one time or another. Vincent Van Gogh was a Dutch post-impressionistic painter and considered among the most famous figures in Western art history. Yet that wasn't always the case. Van Gogh struggled for his work to be recognized. One of his famous paintings, "Starry Night," depicts the moon and stars—eleven of them—surrounded by halos of light. A church steeple towers above the picturesque town in silhouette. Some art critics say the story of Joseph in Genesis 37:9 inspired the painting: *"Then he dreamed another dream and told it to his brothers and said, 'Behold, I have dreamed another dream. Behold, the sun, the moon, and eleven stars were bowing down to me.'"*

The argument is that Van Gogh identified with Joseph. Those eleven stars represent Joseph's eleven brothers who didn't take notice of Joseph and even left him for dead. Ironically, Van Gogh failed to receive the recognition of the art critics of his day, just like Joseph. You may even remember the song *Vincent* by Don McLean, which characterized this dichotomy. Van Gogh's story did not end well. He was shot, and it was rumored he took his own life.

Friends, we all occupy space. That space is validating and sacred in and of itself. But the enemy loves to entice us to second guess ourselves through comparison - by what we do - instead of acknowledgement of our sacred space. Why are we enticed to want more than that? Isn't the world's stardom fleeting?

Not all it seems

Have you ever wondered how to get a star on the Hollywood Walk of Fame? Well, it costs. From what I understand from my limited research, anyone can apply to have a star on the walk as long as you have a fan base of over 10,000 in one of five categories: film, TV, radio, recording, or theatre/live performance. Of those 10,000, twenty-five percent need to be willing to attend the dedication, and you have to pay a sum of five figures for the star itself. A committee decides if you meet the criteria or not. I guess that means you have to be a star before you can have a star. Not at all like it seems.

Carnegie Hall is a classical musician's claim to fame. When I first told my Mom I wanted to be a professional clarinetist, she kept

Chapter 4 – A Star is Born

bragging to everyone how I would play in Carnegie Hall someday. As years went by and my career developed, I discovered three potential paths to perform at Carnegie. The first was to be invited to perform on their series. Second, was to be part of an ensemble scheduled there. Third, you could pay to rent the hall. I wasn't a big enough star to receive an invitation, nor did I have resources to rent, but I actually did get the chance to perform there as part of a musical ensemble. Did the experience satisfy?

Yes, but not in the way you might expect. As I entered the stage, I couldn't help but think about Mom, stardom, and fame. I was reminded to come to terms that I hadn't reached the level of fame I thought I wanted. As I played my first note in the hall, I could sense my sound effortlessly filling up the space. This was my moment, my space. Although Mom passed away years before, I swear I could see her smiling in the audience. In her mind, I made it. I was a star. In my mind, I cherished the moment. The space. I felt like a star. My divine space enjoying a special place.

Lengths

By acknowledging our divine space, could it change our ambitions? Although my personal ambitions weren't to be famous, to what length will we go to be noticed?

A young woman, recently graduating from college, moved to New York City in search of Instagram stardom. Her claim to fame was to showcase fashion in New York City. She desired to show followers what it was like to live the dream. She spent over $10,000 on clothing in less than a year to post pictures of her fashion style. Although she did get some temporary attention, it cost her. She ended up having to get a regular job which took her years to pay off the debt. For what was she searching?

One might say our enemy, Lucifer, originated the idea of "fame" the minute he desired worship for himself. Lucifer is considered a star. It's interesting to note that both Satan and Jesus are called The Morning Star. The difference is that in Isaiah 14:12, Satan's stardom is temporary, because he falls: *How you are fallen from heaven, O Day Star, son of Dawn! How you are cut down to the ground, you who laid the nations low!* In Revelation 22:16, Jesus is referred to as the Morning Star as well, but He is considered the root, a star that doesn't fall: *"I, Jesus, have sent my angel to testify to you about these things for the churches. I am the root and the descendant of David, the bright morning star."*

It's easy for any of us to get caught up in the world's view of stardom. Paul tells us how the church at Corinth caught the celebrity bug. Ironically, they started a competition to determine who was a bigger star, Paul or Apollo. Doesn't competition invite comparison? Paul encouraged them to turn their focus away from the person with the gift and further explained the *purpose* of the gifts we receive—to share the message of Christ. Paul or Apollo didn't do anything to receive their gifts. Instead, Paul encouraged the church to focus on the giver of the gift, God, and His message, not the messenger. He implored them to build each other up, instead of tearing each other down.1 Corinthians 4:1-2 describes this: *"This is how one should regard us, as servants of Christ and stewards of the mysteries of God. Moreover, it is required of stewards that they be found faithful."*

Stars need to shine

If God is trusting us to build up the kingdom with what He's given us, why do we feel it is unfair when He gives someone else more overt talents than ours? Our questions may lie in the differences between talents and spiritual gifts.

Chapter 4 – A Star is Born

Glory Dy explains in her article on Christianity.com, *What is the Difference Between Talent and Spiritual Gifts?* "The difference between spiritual gifts and natural talents is very obvious. Spiritual gifts are received, are given only to those who are saved and are given in surprise and maturity and are used solely for the command of the Church, while natural talents are inherited, can be received by those who are not saved as well, and can be used even for selfish and personal gains."

The challenge we all face is how to integrate our talents with our spiritual gifts. Maybe you want to be a worship leader, pastor, or an author. What gifts or talents do you bring to the table? What is your motive? Talents, no matter how great, if not submitted to the Spirit, cannot produce spiritual fruit. At the same time, talents that aren't utilized can't benefit anyone. Perhaps you're someone who hides your talents to keep from appearing 'self-promoting' since in Christian circles, self-promotion is characterized as selfish. Does that mean God is against us being stars?

The answer is a resounding no. The fact that your body takes up space means you have value and a place of space in the universe. You are a star, designed to reflect His light. When you are born again, and go through the transformation process, your dross will rise, purifying your talents and gifts to be prepared to shine, but not with the temporary stardom that doesn't satisfy. We become stars that shine for Him… not only now, but for eternity.

Platforms

We can't talk about stardom without discussing platform. How big our platform is may distract us from the mission, especially if we start comparing. Take a look at many of our Christian celebrities like Carrie Underwood or Denzel Washington, or athletes like Kirk Cousins, Tim Tebow or Stephen Curry. They have bigger platforms.

It may be in a different sphere of influence (galaxy) than ours, but their lives touch people who need Jesus too. God uniquely equipped them with the talents they need to reach people in that community. Talents, when surrendered to the gifts of the Spirit, can be used to reach whomever God places in front of you.

Friends, we live in a troubled world. Society needs Christians to light the way of truth through words and actions. We do this by running after whatever pleases God. By finding our satisfaction in the Ultimate Star, the one who is rooted and doesn't fall, God sets us apart, equipping us to become stars to a depraved generation. Philippians 2:14-15 explains it this way: *"Do all things without grumbling or disputing, that you may be blameless and innocent, children of God without blemish in the midst of a crooked and twisted generation, among whom you shine as lights in the world."*

We also need to be mindful, that the rooted star shines more brightly than all the others. Jesus Christ is seated at the right hand of God Himself. Christ's standards for stardom, and standards He exhibited for us, are highlighted in Matthew 23:12: *"Whoever exalts himself will be humbled, and whoever humbles himself will be exalted."* If you ever wonder if the humble ways you serve are noticed, even on a smaller platform, they are. I encourage you to Google the lyrics to the song by Larnelle Harris, "I Want to be a Star." The lyrics explain how each time you share the message of Jesus, you are one of His stars, shining brightly for Him.

If indeed we are stars, designed to spread the light of God, why not start with the Gospel? John Mott, an evangelist, and long-time leader of the YMCA, soberly reminds us, "It is a startling and solemnizing fact that even as late as the twentieth century, the Great Command of Jesus Christ to carry the Gospel to all mankind is still so largely unfulfilled."

Chapter 4 – A Star is Born

Friends, until Christ returns, you are the star to fulfill a facet of the mission in your sphere of influence. Our world needs the message of the Gospel. So, shine wherever God has placed you. Who knows, maybe you'll even end up with a fan club.

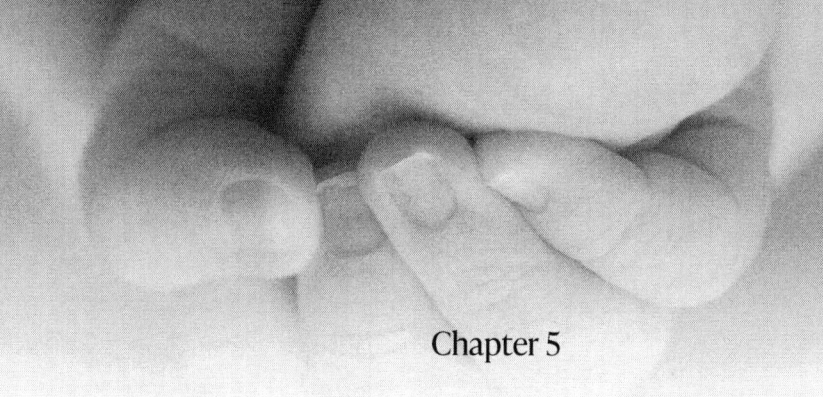

Chapter 5

THE FAN CLUB

———————— " ————————

*The question is not if a man is seeking validation.
The question is, where is he seeking validation from?*
—**Unknown**

*The need to be seen, to be heard, to be
understood, is simply to be human.*
—**L.R. Knost**

Refrigerator art…if you have a young child, pages from coloring books, art projects, or school papers may fill up your refrigerator doors. Indeed, art is for all, but doesn't kid art showcase the warmest childhood memories? Pablo Picasso even made an affirming statement when he said: "Every child is an artist. The problem is how to remain an artist once we grow up."

For that reason and many more, I love kid art. My daughters are adults now, but one picture painted by my then six-year-old daughter still hangs in my home. This image, entitled "Under the Sea," depicts the ocean floor, complete with lobster, fish, snails, and sea urchins.

The painting is so adorable, I had it framed, and it hangs on the blue wall in my home office. When I look at this picture, I see my wide-eyed little girl. I hear her cute voice and sense her childlike presence. When my older daughter was eight, she created pottery. The small, striped, ceramic cup currently holds paper clips. The container is colorful, purposeful, and creative, just like her. When I look at it, it brings a smile to my face. It makes me feel like Mister Rogers.

Looking at these creations—and getting excited about them—reminds me of a crucial role I play in my children's lives. I'm president of their fan club. As a parent, I couldn't help it. Each word, movement, or achievement was cause for celebration. We even celebrated when they went potty in the big potty! Although a parent's job description seems endless, for me, I believed the most significant gift I could give my daughters was to validate and affirm. Perhaps it was because I didn't receive that kind of validation when I was a child, but it also came easily to me because I enjoy them! Through the years, I loved celebrating milestones, achievements, and emphasizing their unique space in the world. Who can forget organizing the pictures and awards for their senior high school open house?

One day, before they graduated, I was picking them up from school and unexpectedly ran into one of their teachers. As our conversation progressed, he described my daughters as two of the most confident students he'd ever encountered. He explained how so many high school students flounder trying to figure out who they are. I was glad someone noticed my intent! With the utmost humility, I thanked him, hoping it meant I filled my role successfully. But what if I didn't? Or what about the times I wasn't enough or too much? Could someone else step in as president of their fan club? As adults, do we even need a fan club?

Most of us equate fan clubs with children or celebrities. After all, "stars" aren't like us. They typically have exceptional charisma, talent, or beauty, which sets them apart. Perhaps we don't feel talented or beautiful enough to warrant a fan club in our ordinary worlds, so we don't bother to give it a thought. Perhaps we don't even think of ourselves as stars.

But friends, God sees us differently. First, as we discovered in the last chapter, we occupy divine space. But He also created us with a longing for a relationship. Naturally, this leaves us propelled to find someone to notice us so we can be in a relationship with them. Isn't wanting to have someone be an eyewitness to our life one of the biggest motivators for marriage?

Think of someone you know who is pregnant. Don't we celebrate the baby before the baby is born? Once we're born, God gives us our instant eyewitness—our parents—who ideally become our fan club. As we grow, our eyewitnesses expand to include grandparents, extended family, friends, and teachers. Ideally, this inherited fan club satisfies our need for validation and affirmation. They hang our artwork on refrigerators and get excited when we take our first step. They attend our sporting events and concerts, support us when we're down, and celebrate our birthday. In a perfect world, they supply the validation and affirmation we were created to need. And in many cases, they may not even be aware they are doing it!

The deficit

Unfortunately, we don't live in a perfect world and may not receive that kind of attention. As a child, perhaps you felt ignored when you tried to share your feelings with your parents but were talked out of your experience or told you should feel something different. Worse yet, when conflict arose, you may not have gotten a chance to explain your perspective and may have ended up being accused or punished for something you didn't do. This type of neglect doesn't feel like a fan club. Instead, it feels like unfair treatment, and left unchecked, can manifest itself in our adult lives. As we get older, we may end up searching to fill that deficit.

If that's you, I'm not sure why your fan club wasn't functional. A defective fan club occurs for many complicated reasons. Perhaps your parents didn't receive validation or affirmation themselves and didn't know how to give it to you. Maybe they were so preoccupied with life's troubles or meeting their own needs that nothing was left for you.

This happened to me. My dad was continually sick, so we were frequently at the hospital. This left little time for me. Mom tried to compensate by affirming me, but when she did, her complimentary words felt like flattery because they didn't meet my basic need—acknowledgement and undivided attention. When I was ten, my father died, which also left me with a deficit. To this day, I cry at the daddy daughter dance at weddings. I also recall hearing a story of a middle child whose younger brother had special needs. Her family was so overwhelmed with taking care of those needs, they didn't realize their daughter felt unnoticed. Or perhaps your fan club was more of a correction club. How heartbreaking. If we're not celebrated, a deficit arises, leaving us feeling empty.

Unfortunately, with a missing or defective fan club, we can feel like orphans. As orphans, we search to find someone, anyone to take notice, or we struggle to get the notice of our parents. As we grow, we cling to others who give us even a little bit of affirmation. Grandparents, friends, peers, teachers, coaches, pastors, talents, or busyness become our fan clubs. If we're still left feeling unseen, we escape by numbing ourselves or strive to do something special to be seen. The striving typically begins with over-achievement, in hopes that it will provide approval from our defective fan club. Good grades, making the all-star team, or getting into a prestigious college are often avenues we explore. If that doesn't satisfy, we may respond by doing nothing or playing the victim, draining others by avoiding life's rigors.

If the need is still not met, we seek out validation and affirmation from other sources. Affairs, drugs, pornography, alcohol, and other addictions are based on a deep need for validation.

Still others try to ignore the need. They may say, "It's all water under the bridge. Why bring it up now? I don't need anyone's attention." Friends, you can't change the fact that your fan club didn't deliver, but I would caution you not to ignore it. The deficit doesn't go away because you don't want to think about it. God created us for relationship. As we see in subsequent chapters, unmet needs rise to the surface. This is the dross. Not having a fan club could be one of your unmet needs. Healing comes when we let the dross rise.

Celebrating each other

In a perfect world, what would it feel like to be celebrated? Is it more than just birthday cake? Do we need awards, trophies, or medals? We can't properly understand how to celebrate each other without reminding ourselves of the differences between validation and affirmation. With that information, we can better determine how much deficit we have or figure out how we can provide for others.

We explained that validation is acknowledgment. When we acknowledge someone or someone's experiences, we tell them they have the right to their experience. Validation is crucial because acknowledgment supports God's divine establishment principle of free will. Since God honors our free will, we must honor another person's right to their perspective—their divine space—even if it's different from ours. Listening is one of the best ways to validate, but it doesn't mean we have to agree or view that person's experience in the same way.

One of the best listening skills to show someone validation is to do what communication experts call "reflecting." If we do this properly, we paraphrase what the other person said. When we repeat their feelings back to them, they feel heard. When we reflect correctly, we are not trying to talk someone out of their experience. Instead, we acknowledge they have a human right to make their own choices and have their own perspective. Just like trees, streams, or any other living thing, we occupy space in this world. No one else can take up our sacred space. Validation doesn't offer judgment; it merely acknowledges. I recall when I was a kid, I would tell my mom "My finger hurts when I do this." Her response was, "Well, just don't do that." Honestly, I didn't feel acknowledged in that moment.

Affirmation is different. Although affirmation may acknowledge, it goes a step further by communicating approval. Words of affirmation are positive and life-giving and make us feel celebrated! Compliments, a card in the mail, a gift, or serving, shows notice.

So yes, go ahead and celebrate! Put your three-year-old son's drawing on the refrigerator. Doing so validates his space in the world. If you want to take it further and affirm him, tell him what you like about his picture. This affirms the action. To take it further and affirm him as a person, show approval of something truly unique in the picture that reflects his soul.

Expectations

Now that you've read these definitions, can you say you received adequate validation or affirmation from your fan club? Were your expectations realistic?

Since we live in sin-filled world, expect some deficit. As adults, we can look back and speculate why. An excellent way to measure your need is to ask yourself the following question: Do you assume someone doesn't love you if they don't agree with you?

Chapter 5 – The Fan Club

In my counseling experience, I've seen clients on both sides of the seesaw when I ask this question. Think about it. Would someone who truly felt validated be concerned if the other person agreed with them or not? Can we live without celebration if we receive acknowledgment? Conflict may arise in the expectation.

Deep down, as adults, we need someone, anyone, to acknowledge our space, and our experience. We also need someone to celebrate us. However, as we mature, the need sits in our subconscious, or gets cleverly disguised. Since we don't have temper tantrums anymore to get noticed, what can we expect?

The God who sees

Since we were created for relationship, God wants us to know we are seen. Yes, He supplies others to help satisfy our need, but if we look strictly to them and forget about God, we cause ourselves problems. Let's take a look at one of our Bible heroes, David, through the eyes of validation and affirmation.

When he was young, one could say David didn't have much of a fan club. His father didn't even tell the king he had a son named David. David's brothers thought he was crazy for saying he was called by God to be king and to fight the giant. King Saul even doubted the young shepherd. Not much validation there, and certainly no affirmation.

Jump ahead a few years. As an adult, David committed some serious sins. Let's analyze David's interest in Bathsheba. We might conclude David used her as a way to feel validated which is what most affairs reveal. (We'd probably have to ask David's counselor about that.) One simple act resulted in a chain of events, including murder! Could part of his struggle be related to David's unresolved deficit? It's interesting to note that as David went into exile, there was a lot of pleading with God for validation.

As we read the Psalms, we see two sides of David—the human who needed deliverance, and the man chasing after God's heart. What was David searching for? Most of the Psalms show David's laments and desperate cries for God to notice him. Each Psalm showcases a different experience of David. As we reach Psalm 139:1-10, something changes. We see how David begins to understand the purest source of validation.

> *O LORD, you have searched me and known me!*
> *You know when I sit down and when I rise up;*
> *you discern my thoughts from afar.*
> *You search out my path and my lying down*
> *and are acquainted with all my ways.*
> *Even before a word is on my tongue,*
> *behold, O LORD, you know it altogether.*
>
> *You hem me in, behind and before,*
> *and lay your hand upon me.*
> *Such knowledge is too wonderful for me;*
> *it is high; I cannot attain it.*
>
> *Where shall I go from your Spirit?*
> *Or where shall I flee from your presence?*
> *If I ascend to heaven, you are there!*
> *If I make my bed in Sheol, you are there!*
> *If I take the wings of the morning*
> *and dwell in the uttermost parts of the sea,*
> *even there your hand shall lead me,*
> *and your right hand shall hold me.*

Chapter 5 – The Fan Club

Friends, the kind of detailed attention God describes in this Psalm is far above what any other fan club can give you! He is with you twenty-four-seven, so no matter what you're going through, He's there. And if that's not enough, God takes it a step further. He actually *pursues* you! Psalm 23:5 tells us: *"Surely goodness and mercy shall follow me all the days of my life."* I discovered the root word for *follow* is actually *pursue*. The verse now reads: *Surely goodness and mercy shall pursue me all the days of my life.* So, yes, God notices you. His goodness and mercy pursue you. You can't get much more noticed than that! Can you see it?

If you haven't felt pursued by God, my prayer is that you will view your space in the world as God sees it—sacred. Even if your fan club was faulty, or you don't feel like a star, remember He sees everything about you. No matter what facet you look at this from, you can't escape His presence. Psalms 37:5-6 (MSG) tells us, *"Open up before God, keep nothing back; he'll do whatever needs to be done: He'll validate your life in the clear light of day and stamp you with approval at high noon."*

Friends, He validates you by His mercy which grants you access to His presence. He is always here, right with you.

LISTEN TO: You are Here

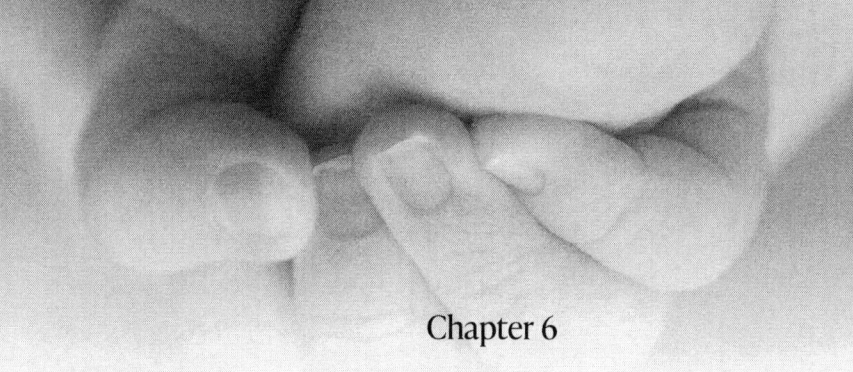

Chapter 6

FACETS

*Most of all, differences of opinion are
opportunities for learning.*
—Terry Tempest Williams

*...But I'm annoying you to no purpose with my
arguments. A person whose house is only open on
the west can't see the sunrise at dawn; it's only seen
when the sun sets at dusk.*

*If one compares the color and appearance of
the two, one will argue forever...The fault lies not
with the vision but with the closed windows.
If you look out of only one opening till the day
you die, you'll never see anything new.*
—Saratchandra Chattopadhyay

*We do not see things as they are,
we see things as we are.*
—Anais Nin

A Firm GRASP

It wasn't the safest place to grow up. The racially tense, low socio-economic neighborhood in northwest Detroit was filled with fatherless families, adopted children, troubled teens, drugs, and neglected elderly. Break-ins, arson, racial incidents, and fistfights were rampant. As a means of self-protection, we scoped out neighbors carefully, using street smarts in our evaluation.

Aside from physical safety, basic survival needs were a big concern. Having enough money to pay rent, pay utilities, and buy groceries were priorities. Food stamps and handouts were common. For complicated reasons, contact with extended family was rare, so a few elderly people in the neighborhood tried to take us under their wings as surrogate grandparents. One of my fondest childhood memories was spending time with a lovely older woman who lived next door. She introduced me to tea parties and taught me how to knit. God provided her to be part of my extended fan club.

These were the days of playing in the neighborhood freely and heading in when the streetlights came on. Despite our troubles, we wanted to know our neighbors. In a small, grey house down the block lived a retired couple. I often found the woman outside tending to flowers and the gentleman tinkering in his garage. Precisely organized throughout the wood shelves were rock tumblers, geodes, gemstones, and jars filled with stones. Rocks and gemstones weren't just a hobby for him; they were his passion. He encouraged us to find special rocks so he could polish them. When I finally brought him some rocks, I became fascinated by how much the stones changed after polishing. I didn't realize there were so many colors to uncover!

I can still remember how much his face lit up like a Christmas tree with every opportunity he had to teach us. We learned about the polishing process and how facets are the special way gemstones are cut. Facets can be produced in many shapes and sizes and are generally arranged in groups depending on the gem material. When

Chapter 6 – Facets

cut just right, the angle plays a crucial role in attracting light, with reflecting light being the ultimate goal.

I never thought about facets again until I got engaged. As I looked at my diamond ring, I enjoyed playing with the facets, attempting to catch the light. After further examination, I became intrigued. These angles needed to be precisely cut to reflect the light, but they didn't reflect light all the time. The moment you moved the stone, another facet would catch the light source. I enjoyed playing with the light and the facets. As I examined my diamond closer, I couldn't help but reflect on how God must look at us as facets. If indeed we are stars, with facets, when cut just right, we will reflect light—the light of the Master.

Perspectives

Using this illustration, it's important to remember that one facet is one angle, catching the light from one particular viewpoint. One facet doesn't reflect ALL the light. Since each of us hold a slightly different perspective of the world based on our experiences, we may have to move things around a little to catch the light because our perspectives aren't always pure. Our viewpoints may be based on negative messages received from our past, celebrations missed, fan club deficits, or our own problem-solving methods.

Let me share a simple example. My father was handicapped and in a wheelchair. Because of that experience, one might say I have a unique perspective, or facet, regarding handicapped individuals. Because of my experience, isn't it possible I might have stronger opinions about handicapped parking spaces than someone who didn't have the same experience? Even to this day, each time I see someone parking in a handicapped spot when they aren't handicapped, I'm reminded of how much those parking spots might have meant to Dad. Another person might understand and acknowledge my perspective, offering empathy, but not everyone else will see it the same way I do. It's entirely possible I am more passionate about it than others because I've had a different experience.

There are also times a group of individuals may have the same experience but view it differently. When I was ten, my Dad died, and my brothers were twelve, thirteen, and fourteen. All five of us viewed Dad's death from different facets and had different responses as a result. Mom was lonely, I felt unprotected, and my brothers grieved the loss of Dad's guidance, provision, and discipline. Same experience, different facets.

This Is Us, a popular television program, displays facets well. In each episode, the writers focus on one incident that happens to the family. As the audience, we get to be eyewitnesses to the incident from the different facets of each family member. We get a glimpse of each person's state of mind and emotional state leading up to the incident, what they experienced during the incident, and how it affected them afterwards. We begin to understand a little more about that person. It reminds us there is always more to a story than we can personally see.

Although it makes for good TV and helps us look at experiences through other's eyes, it can sometimes leave us feeling uneasy when human experiences are interpreted differently. We may question ourselves, wondering if our viewpoint is skewed. This is typically a time where we need acknowledgment. If someone doesn't view something the exact same way I do, does that make me wrong? Does it make them wrong? Does anyone have to be wrong?

For a season of my life, I was troubled by facets. Since I didn't feel acknowledged, I took offense when others didn't see the world the same way I saw it. After all, my fan club was defective, I wasn't a big star, and due to my abuse, I wanted to right the wrongs. In my mind, my world view was superior because no one understood my need for justice or could possibly see things from my perspective. If I'm really honest, it was pride. After all, being right gave me power and confidence to justify the validation and affirmation I craved. But all this did was cause problems in my relationships.

Ironically, in my fight for my voice, I felt unheard. This made me emotionally domineering as I put other's perspectives on trial. After all, it was up to me to deliver the truth. The danger in knowing a little scripture is knowing a little truth. By presenting things from God's perspective, the facet I saw must be right. Is there a Pharisee in the room?

Fellow believers, the enemy tempts us to do the same thing. Because Jesus is the Way, the Truth, and the Life, we believe we are privy to the correct facet. Of course, we want to anchor our beliefs in truth and see things as God sees them. Good results come from obedience. But we may be walking down a slippery slope. Are we really capable of viewing life from God's perspective? Do we really know God's thoughts? Isaiah 55:8-9 tells us: *"For my thoughts are not your thoughts, neither are your ways my ways, declares the Lord. For as the heavens are higher than the earth, so are my ways higher than your ways and my thoughts than your thoughts."*

Friends, as I've grown, I'm convinced that it isn't up to me to make others see the truth. I can communicate truth, and I can send a message, but I can't make someone accept it. That's the job of the Holy Spirit. During this particular season of my life, I wasn't in a place where I could consider the facets others saw. I couldn't possibly validate others, because I was too consumed with seeking validation for myself.

Free will

Seeking validation for ourselves may keep us from respecting others. We can't talk about respect without bringing up free will. As one of

God's divine establishment principles, everyone gets to choose. Jesus implies the concept of choice in John 7:17 when He says, *"Anyone who chooses to do the will of God will find out whether my teaching comes from God or whether I speak on my own."* Friends, we get to choose. We choose for God. We choose against God. We choose our viewpoint, or we choose to ignore someone else's. We choose how we will respond to a situation, and how we will express it. To truly respect others, we need to honor their facets.

What caused problems for me is when I would offer my perspective even though no one asked. Growing up without a Dad, being sexually abused, and physically assaulted, probably leaves me with a stronger need to be heard than others. But at the heart of it, I needed validation. At that time, I wasn't self-aware enough to realize that everyone has different facets, and only God can see all the facets of any one situation or person. I wasn't aware enough to notice God "cutting" the stone so that I could shine and be a multi-faceted reflection of His light. The bottom line is I lacked respect for God because I didn't honor the divine space He provided all of us.

To respect God's divine institution of free will, we must embrace our perspective while validating someone else's right to theirs. Friends, I can't say this enough. We all have different experiences and different perspectives about those experiences. Because of free will, sowing and reaping will follow our choices, but it's still important to accept everyone else's right to make those choices, even if we don't agree with them.

As an example, suppose you are a detective interviewing a man who committed murder. The man tries to explain why he did what he did. To the murderer, his perspective makes complete sense. He had a terrible childhood and an addiction which led to his decision. That's his perspective—one facet of the situation. As the detective taking notes, you can validate (acknowledge) what the man believes or sees about the situation without giving him affirmation (approval). Believe it or not, even someone who commits murder has a right to express his perspective. It doesn't mean there won't be sowing and reaping to his choice. But living a life of mercy allows this man the right to his viewpoint, even if it's skewed, or evil.

Opinions

As we dig deeper into this concept of facets, how we express our facet involves opinions. I admit I'm not perfect at this, but when we validate someone, it's important to wait or ask permission to offer our perspective in return. Most people don't feel validated if we offer our perspective while they are expressing theirs.

Webster's definition of opinion tells us that an opinion is a subjective belief, judgment or perspective that a person has formed about a topic, issue, person or thing that is not conclusive. Why aren't opinions conclusive? Perhaps it's because one person can't see a situation from all facets. Our opinions aren't always based on a complete perspective, and often they're not based on God's perspective either.

A great debate happening in our country involves fake news. With the onset of social media, we receive so many different facets of the same information. It's challenging to know if all perspectives are based on the entire truth. We're learning more and more that media is limiting our right to see all facets. Could those presenting information be developing their viewpoint from a limited perspective or bias? Does any one person really know all the facts? Who sees things from every facet?

If you don't know whether you struggle in this area, here's a question to consider. If you express your opinion and someone disagrees, how do you respond?

Confidence

As we accept our need for validation, understand our divine space, and the condition of our fan club, our confidence about our facet builds. Authentic confidence births when we become self-aware enough to recognize the strengths and weaknesses of our facet. As we mature in Christ, we see how God affirms our facet and is lovingly "cutting" our facet to reflect His light. We also see when our facets may be skewed. We can have confidence in validating others.

If we are ready to validate someone's right to their experience without shaming or bullying them, then we should feel confident enough to express our opinion. However, this doesn't mean we should demand our right to share our facet or insist our facet is the only perspective. Otherwise, others may lose confidence in us.

As I personally struggled during this part of my transformation, God revealed to me seven different ways to express my facets, and respect the facets of others.

1) **Viewpoints change.** Everyone views life differently, but our views change as we mature. We may have strong opinions about something, only to discover years later that our viewpoint was skewed. Since that happens to us, we can expect it to happen to others. 1 Corinthians 13:12 (MSG) explains it best: *"We don't yet see things clearly. We're squinting in a fog, peering through a mist. But it won't be long before the weather clears, and the sun shines bright! We'll see it all then, see it all as clearly as God sees us, knowing him directly just as he knows us!"*

2) **Validation goes a long way towards a softened heart.** As previously mentioned, when we validate someone, we acknowledge their divine space and their experience. By reflecting back, others feel heard. If they feel heard, they are more willing to listen to your facet. God is the only one who sees everything from every facet and is in

the heart-softening business. 1 Samuel 16:7 tells us, *"Do not look on his appearance or on the height of his stature, because I have rejected him. For the Lord sees not as man sees. Man looks on the outward appearance, but the Lord looks on the heart."*

3) **Admonishment requires validation and affirmation.** We are not to correct or attempt to change a non-believer's viewpoint except when sharing the Gospel. 1 Corinthians 2:14 explains: *"The natural person does not accept the things of the Spirit of God, for they are folly to him, and he is not able to understand them because they are spiritually discerned."*

Admonishment (warning) is primarily between believers. When we admonish our brothers or sisters in Christ, we must approach them from a place of love. We must try to validate their perspective. Try this sequence: validate, admonish, affirm. Be careful not to affirm too much, or it may come across as patronizing. Start by giving other believers the benefit of the doubt. Romans 15:14 tells us: *"I myself am satisfied about you, my brothers, that you yourselves are full of goodness, filled with all knowledge and able to instruct one another."*

4) **Inadequacy breeds dissension.** If our perspective comes from our own feelings of inadequacy, shame, vows we made, or some message from our past, our view isn't pure. We are no longer offering our unique perspective which reflects the light. Instead, we offer defensiveness, leading to dissension. Romans 12:18 explains: *"If possible, so far as it depends on you, live peaceably with all."*

5) **Be careful about those messages.** According to Maxwell Maltz, author of *Psycho-Cybernetics*, reprogramming your mind requires a message from an authoritative source, repeated with intensity. If you feel bad about yourself because you are too easily swayed by others' opinions, surrendering to the Spirit by reciting Scripture to yourself can help you hold on to the proper, truthful perspective and see others' views in the right light. Psalm 119:15-16

comforts us: *"I will meditate on your precepts and fix my eyes on your ways. I will delight in your statutes; I will not forget your word."* When we live a life of mercy, we understand validation comes at the cross.

6) **God has many facets. Each of us reflects a facet of God.** When we look at God's attributes, we can't help but notice His many facets. He is love, yet righteous. He is fair, yet kind. He is mighty, yet merciful. Each one of us on any given day may reflect a different facet of God through the fruit of the Spirit. This is our star shining. I can't wait to get to heaven and see Him in all His glory, with every facet shining! Though we don't know what He will look like, Revelation 1:14-16 gives us a little glimpse: *"The hairs of his head were white, like white wool, like snow. His eyes were like a flame of fire, his feet were like burnished bronze, refined in a furnace, and his voice was like the roar of many waters. In his right hand, he held seven stars, from his mouth came a sharp two-edged sword, and his face was like the sun shining in full strength."*

7) **God notices you.** God is the supreme being who sees all. His view is way bigger than any of ours. He notices each one of us. Haggar referred to God as EL ROI—the God who sees. She discovered He intimately knew the details of her situation, caring for her, and giving her hope.

As I began to utilize these points, something changed. I started to show others more respect, which started by embracing the facets of others. I discovered the more facets there are, the better. Then more of God's light is reflected!

By acknowledging God first, we begin to see both ourselves and others differently. Successful relationships with self, others, and understanding facets can bring empathy, compassion and ultimately, mercy, to any relationship. We become more open to new discoveries. Psalms 115:1 sums it up: *"Not to us, O Lord, not to us, but*

Chapter 6 – Facets

to your name give glory, for the sake of your steadfast love and your faithfulness!"

When mercy is present in our interactions, mutual respect, vulnerability, and peace are inevitable. May we concern ourselves with being the facet which best reflects His light.

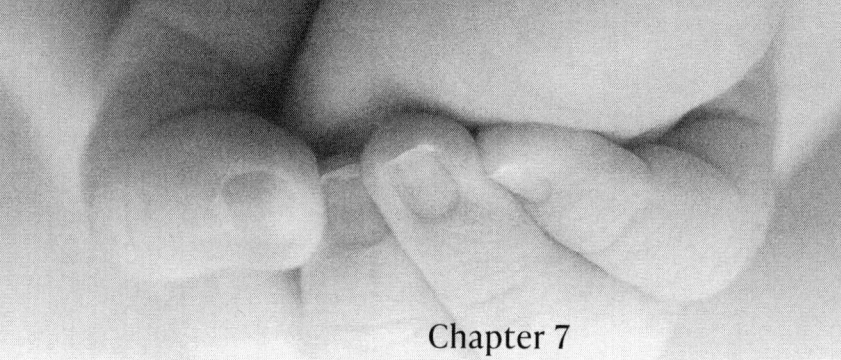

Chapter 7

THE FRAME

"

*A foundational issue in getting to
know ourselves has to do with going back,
understanding how our families and cultures
have shaped us into who we are today.*
–Peter Scherzzo, Emotionally Healthy Spirituality

Forget the former things; do not dwell on the past.
–Isaiah 43:18 (NIV)

Walking through a museum of art, one can't help but notice the tall ceilings, white walls, and wide-open spaces. Sculptures, paintings, photography, printmaking, and glass blowing stimulate our senses. We appreciate art for its beauty of line, symmetry, and color. Even how art is displayed is part of the experience. Art also represents and reflects our culture and human nature. Remarkably, two people can look at the same piece of art and have different responses. Sometimes when others see something in a work that we don't, it challenges us. Art expands.

A Firm GRASP

On one particular sun-filled, laissez-faire kind of day, I found myself in the section of an art museum that included enormous paintings. Many were portraits that could fill up an entire wall in my home. Aside from their size, the frames intrigued me. Gold-laden, intricate, and ornate, they seemed to make quite the statement. Sometimes all I could see was the large frame. Other times, the art overpowered the frame. It was interesting to note how the frame altered my view of the painting.

I began to wonder whether the artist selects the frame before or after he finishes the painting. Does the frame change the painting? The real masterpiece is the painting, not the frame, yet the frame can be a work of art in itself. Either way, it appears to be an important part of a completed masterpiece.

Using the masterpiece and its frame as an analogy, do you see yourself as God's work of art? Is the frame part of the masterpiece? Scripture tells us in Ephesians 2:10 (NLT), *"For we are God's masterpiece. He has created us anew in Christ Jesus, so we can do the good things he planned for us long ago."*

This verse tells the who, the what, and the why. Who we are is God's masterpiece. What He's done is create us anew. Why does He do it? So, we can do the good things He planned. Understanding we are a masterpiece satisfies identity issues. Being "created anew" means we don't have to live through messages of our past. The "good things He planned for us" tells us we have a purpose…a mission.

If our mission is to present ourselves as God's masterpiece, then a frame is implied. While frames can be works of art themselves, they should never overshadow or overpower the painting. Using this analogy, the frame symbolizes the things from our past that we didn't have any control over—like what town we were born in, our parents, our siblings, etc., and the messages they left us. Did our fan club make us feel like masterpieces? Do those messages from our past overshadow or keep us from creating our masterpiece?

Message Default System (MDR)

Our fan club told us a lot about ourselves. We either received messages through acknowledgment and celebration, or through correction or punishment. We learned about limitations, mistakes and sin and how it challenges us to see ourselves in a positive light. Deep down, as sinners, we know we are unworthy. But we don't like feeling that way.

Struggling to suppress those feelings, we swing like a pendulum, reeling between two opposite views. One day, we think we're amazing; the other, we believe we aren't worthy. Many of those internal messages may not be obvious to us. Instead, they become 'meta-messages'—a personal message that is implied or inferred from an overlying message.

Meta-messages infiltrate our thoughts and can affect how we feel about ourselves. They may be motivated by vows, shame, or feelings of inadequacies. Instead of fighting these messages, sometimes we simply default to them, which I call the Message Default System (MDS). These negative messages come from the frame we didn't get to choose. The frame that includes our family of origin, defective fan club or skewed facet.

Condition

As you reflect on your frame, what condition is it in? What meta-messages have you received or failed to retract? Some frames may be simple, ornate or intact; but most are dull, broken, or wounded. Wounds from our frame rooted in criticism can stay with us for a long time, causing internal damage and distracting us from creating our masterpiece. Here are a few different ways we assess our frame's condition.

1) WHO are you? Identity crisis –If our facet wasn't validated, we become unsure of who we are. We look outwardly to find anyone

to show us how to feel better about our limits, mistakes, and sin. We vacillate between messages of the past and who we want to be, often leaving us stuck.

2) WHAT has power over me? Powerlessness—We feel powerless when we don't get to choose the burdens and issues from the previous generation and its impact on us. We may feel powerless in choosing our careers or who we marry.

Feeling powerless may leave us vacillating like a seesaw. We are up when we take control, or down when we focus on the sins of our fathers. We may be up when we take full responsibility or down when we view our lives through shame. Either way, we put ourselves and others on trial. In order to regain power, we may pursue justice.

3) WHY? Purpose—Our purpose is our motivator. However, if no one made us feel like a star, we may try to overachieve or hide in response. Without affirmation, we lack motivation to create our masterpiece because all we can see is our messed-up frame. We're so busy fixing the frame that we forget about the masterpiece.

In this book, it's important to examine our frame in detail. We become more aware by exploring ways we've responded which didn't satisfy. We learn about cramps, vows, shame, and defensiveness. We look to reframe our Message Default System to a Mercy Default System.

I will warn you. As you analyze your past, you'll have to get real, which means you may discover some messages you believed are actually blatant lies. These lies may make you angry or resentful if you don't denounce them. God refers to this fight as "the good fight." This is about resolving our relationship with self. You'll do that by becoming more self-aware.

The process

Doing our framework is part of the spiritual transformation process, known as sanctification. Sanctification means setting apart. As we examine our frame, we view the world differently. There are three phases to this process: positional sanctification, experiential sanctification and ultimate sanctification.

Positional sanctification is our justification. At salvation, we accept our unworthiness as sinners and become believers, declared righteous because of the work of the cross. Our concept of self turns from sinner to saint by accepting that justification is the work of God and God alone.

Romans 8:1 tells us: *"There is therefore now no condemnation to them that are in Christ Jesus."* If you have not believed Jesus died for your sins, you still can. Confess your sins, accept that Jesus took the punishment for your sins, and turn your life over to God.

Experiential sanctification is the journey towards spiritual maturity. With the goal of Christlikeness, we could call it "progressive" sanctification as the Holy Spirit produces godliness in the life of the believer. During this phase, the believer fluctuates between the old sin nature and the work of the Spirit. This is when the dross rises, and cleansing begins. The tension between the Spirit and the flesh makes us feel like a hybrid.

Romans 12: 2 commands, *"Do not be conformed to this world, but be transformed by the renewal of your mind, that by testing you may discern what is the will of God, what is good and acceptable and perfect."*

If you are a believer in Jesus Christ, this is the stage you're in. Your frame has always existed, but during this stage you are becoming more aware of it, working *through* your salvation, not *for* it. Even though we are no longer condemned, in this phase, we get to learn how to live as an unworthy saint.

Friends, how can we work through our salvation if we haven't identified what we need saving from? We are told in Philippians 2:12 to *"work out your own salvation with fear and trembling."*

Ultimate sanctification is the final stage of sanctification. Realized at the resurrection when the believer will be transformed into the likeness of Christ and presented to the Lord as holy, it includes the redemption of the body, eternal inheritance, and deliverance from the wrath of God. I can't wait! Redemption wins!

Acceptance

As we walk through the experiential phase of sanctification, acceptance of our frame is crucial. Although many of us what to change our frame, acceptance accelerates our transformation. Understanding our frame will help us understand our identity, connect with our power source, and narrow down our purpose. I wouldn't be surprised if you characterize the process as "painfully wonderful." But how do you start? Through self-awareness.

Self-awareness involves examination. How has your past shaped you? What messages did you receive? Are those messages kingdom-focused? In what ways have you responded to today's problems based on your past?

One of the best tools I use in counseling to determine framework is the Lifeline Chart©. The top of the chart identifies positive life events like graduations, making the basketball team, and getting married. My upper half included coming to Jesus, my friendship with music, and the birth of my daughters. The bottom half identifies negative life happenings. For me, the bottom half included sexual abuse, my dad dying when I was ten, and my divorce. Once you complete this Lifeline Chart, you can begin to talk about the messages those life happenings gave you. You can find access to the chart at the back of the book.

Chapter 7 – The Frame

As you work on your Lifeline Chart, I encourage you *not* to complete it alone. Explore your frame with a trusted friend, mentor, or counselor. Reliving painful experiences can be emotionally exhausting. Having someone come alongside you provides encouragement and objectivity. Others may be able to bring out aspects of your past you hadn't considered, or suggest you explore paths you weren't aware needed healing. Choose someone who loves Jesus and is your fan.

As you move forward in the book, other chapters will help you. Use it to identify your motives, vows, and attitudes towards shame. Most important, as you go through the process, be careful not to put yourself or others on trial. Judging is counterproductive to healing. This includes judging yourself.

To stay away from judging, consider the following example. Let's say your mom said, "You can't think straight if you're tired, hungry, or upset." How did you interpret that statement? Did you think you were a failure because you couldn't think straight? Perhaps these kinds of harmful messages were sent to you from broken people or are just the way you feel about yourself.

Keep in mind, personal responsibility will not be ignored during this phase. You may have been raised to be a responsible citizen and accept the consequences of your choices—but even if you weren't raised that way, you are still responsible. Remember, the past is your frame, not your masterpiece. By ignoring your frame, you will continue to feel powerless, questioning your identity, needing excessive validation and affirmation, and being distracted from living your purpose. The only one who wins is the enemy.

Friends, the Holy Spirit will help shed light in those dark places through discernment. When you were a child, your powers of discernment were limited as you trusted adults for truth. However, as you matured, you saw things differently. 1 Corinthians 13:11-12 tells us, *"When I was a child, I spoke like a child, I thought like a child,*

I reasoned like a child. When I became a man, I gave up childish ways. For now, we see in a mirror dimly, but then face to face. Now I know in part; then I shall know fully, even as I have been fully known."

Salvation is your healing. When looking at your past, please don't assume you're doomed. Going through this process is meant to cleanse you. As you learn to live in the dichotomy of feeling unworthy and being a masterpiece at the same time, you will feel a sense of confidence. You'll learn to accept your frame. Do not lose heart. Without acknowledging the wounds from these messages, or clearing up any misunderstandings, you cannot embrace the *depth* of salvation God provides.

In what areas do you need to become more self-aware of your framework?

Framework

Framework leads us to accept most things are out of our control. My framework took me back to my childhood growing up in a low socio-economic, racially tense neighborhood in northwest Detroit. The community and the household made me feel unsafe. Financial issues, medical concerns, the death of my father along with memories of verbal abuse, sexual molestation, and physical violence were painful for me to accept. What happened to my Hallmark movie?

Just as an onion has many layers, each issue is its own layer. I've spent a good deal of my adult life working through these issues and how to respond. It hasn't been easy, but I am grateful for the healing God has provided. When triggers come—and they do—I find myself momentarily jumbled, but not defeated. Putting things into their rightful places—it is what it is—allows me to redirect my facet so I can shine for Jesus.

As you examine your frame, how will you know if you have come to peace with your past? Are you resentful of your limitations?

Do you beat yourself up when you make mistakes? Have you forgiven those who may have neglected to validate or affirm you?

Mercy

Friends, as you look at your frame through the Lifeline Chart, be kind to yourself. When you were a child, you didn't have answers and looked to imperfect people to give you coping skills, some of which may have resulted in addictive behavior, faulty thinking, or sinful patterns. Even though you didn't get to choose your frame, you do get to decide how you will respond. Avoid falling into the trap of inadequacy, making unrealistic vows, or cramping what God is trying to do. The goal isn't to dwell on the past, but to receive validation from your heavenly Father for every pretty or painful element. Think of it all as a gift, wrapped in mercy, designed to help you enjoy the moment.

John Ortberg in his book, *God Is Closer Than You Think,* says, "The greatest moment of your life is now. Not because it's pleasant or happy or easy, but because this moment is the only moment you've got. Every past moment is irretrievably gone. It's never coming back. If you live there, you lose your life. And the future is always out there somewhere. You can spend an eternity waiting for tomorrow or worrying about tomorrow. If you live there, you likewise will lose your life. This moment is God's irreplaceable gift to you."

Take this moment to examine your frame. I'm not sure where this moment will take you, but it's meant to bring glory to God through your masterpiece.

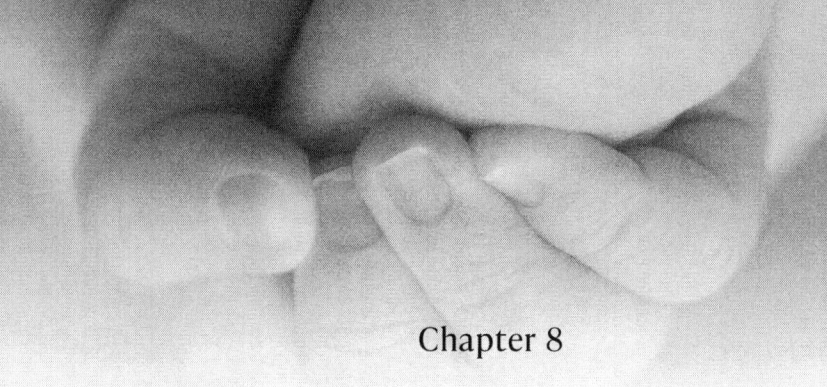

Chapter 8

ENTER THE HALL

———————————   **"**   ———————————

*Shame is the most powerful master emotion.
It's the fear that we're not good enough.
Because true belonging only happens when we
present our authentic, imperfect selves to the world,
our sense of belonging can never be greater
than our level of self-acceptance.*
—**Brené Brown**

Remember when you were a kid? Growing up in Detroit was challenging, but one of my fondest memories was being part of a baseball family. I can recall the smell of ballpark franks at the Detroit Tigers stadium and enjoyed listening to Ernie Harwell's voice on the radio. Aside from being a Tiger fan, impromptu baseball games were common in the streets. I remember my disabled father hitting a few balls to my brothers from his wheelchair and playing games until the streetlights went on. Collecting baseball cards were my brothers' passion and keeping up with players' stats is something they still do today. I enjoyed playing girls' softball, but my brothers, well, they played Little League. Fastpitch. The real deal.

One summer night, my middle brother was scheduled to pitch, and another brother to catch. That in itself was pretty cool, but what transpired became a family triumph. Although I didn't understand it much then, apparently an outstanding baseball game has little to no scoring. It's all about the pitcher, so a no-hitter was really, good baseball.

That night it happened. My brother threw a no-hitter as the pitcher, with my other brother as the catcher. Young boys dream about these kinds of games, and that special night was our family's little "claim to fame."

Boys also dream of making it to the major leagues. The percentages are low, but for my brothers, becoming a Detroit Tiger remained a fantasy. Winning the 1968 World Series is still talked about today and in 1984, all three of my brothers went to a Detroit Tigers World Series game. One of my brothers even participated in a Detroit Tigers Fantasy Camp. I also recall a few road trips to Cooperstown, New York, where they would visit the Baseball Hall of Fame. My brothers loved going to the Hall of Fame, looking at the artifacts and exhibits which showcase their favorite pastime.

The Baseball Hall of Fame has a mission: To preserve the sport's history, honor excellence within the game, and make a connection between the generations of people who enjoy baseball.

It's not easy to be inducted into the Hall of Fame. First, a player must have played at least ten years in the major leagues and been retired for five. The Hall of Fame Board of Directors pick a six-person screening committee, consisting of various sportswriters who have covered major-league baseball for at least ten years to decide on the nominations. Ten candidates are selected from the nominations. Being chosen is a big deal.

A different hall

Let's face it. Most of us will never belong to any Hall of Fame. We're not that big of a deal. Although we are stars, most of us aren't celebrities, a household name, nor will we reach a high level of excellence in one particular field. As we explore our need for validation and affirmation, not having anyone honor us can leave a void. If we haven't achieved, excelled, or been noticed, we feel like a failure. Getting an award, even a simple one, can provide us with affirmation we didn't know we needed. Until we start comparing.

Comparison is like a web. It leaves us feeling either better than or less than. How we compare, may lead us to a different hall—one we enter subconsciously. It's a hall filled with embarrassment. It's a secret hall, and one we don't want others to know about. It's a hall where things we've done wrong, or wrongs others have committed against us, are highlighted and exposed. It's the place where failures are in the forefront and regrets live vibrantly. Enter…the Hall of Shame.

The Hall of Shame has a mission: To preserve our life history, highlight our traumas, dwell on regrets, and potentially reshape memories. In this hall, it isn't about awards we've received, degrees earned, or precious family videos. It is a place where we elevate and showcase the trauma we've experienced, the elephants in the room, and the family secrets. Sometimes the exhibits include our sins or the sin of others. Sometimes it's the way we respond to sin. At one time or another, we all enter this hall, whether we want to or not. Unfortunately, some of us don't just visit, we live there.

The hiding place

Hiding the shame that comes from sin is one of Satan's tactics. He will want you to ignore, hide, or dwell on your shame. Shame is a response to our dross. Until we are aware we have dross, we may not know about the Hall of Shame. Without labeling the dross, there is no purifying. Without purification, there is no reflection of God.

Becoming aware of my Hall of Shame didn't come easily. With so many things happening to me, I didn't want to be pitied or looked at as a victim, so I put my shame in a little compartment in my psyche that I didn't dare open. Not only did I want to forget about my traumatic experiences, I hated being labeled a broken person. The other alternative was to be vulnerable, and that was too risky.

To protect myself, I hid tough memories in that inner compartment I affectionately call the hiding place. I didn't see any reason to re-live the sexual abuse, exploitation, bullying, harassment, verbal abuse, physical abuse, or betrayal. I didn't want to look at those artifacts, let alone honor them. No, thank you, let's just forget about it please.

I hid for decades by choosing to ignore my frame and the messages which came along with them. I didn't see any connection between those artifacts and current events. The thought of paying a counselor and spending hours and hours uncovering the past felt brutal. Aren't I honoring sin by dwelling on it? Can't we just move on?

What I came to realize is validation isn't just to acknowledge our divine space. Even our hurts need to be acknowledged. The family secret, traumatic event, or secret sin can affect our self-concept. Maybe it's the family drunk, abuser, womanizer, porn addict, drug dealer, gambler, enabler, or mentally ill person. Maybe it's the lifestyle we lived before we were saved. Perhaps we don't want to scar the family name so we avoid the elephant in the room and lock it up so no one else can access it. After all, isn't all this self-awareness a prescription for more pain?

Friends, denying the dross, or our response to it, doesn't make it go away. The best way to be cleansed is to allow God to bring everything to the light. By entering the Hall of Shame, we acknowledge the elephants in the room, and start to bury the power they have over us. Brené Brown explains it this way: "You either walk inside your story and own it, or you stand outside your story and hustle for your worthiness."

The hustle

The hustle starts with validation and affirmation. Many of the ways we respond to life events come from the artifacts (triggers) or characters (people) in our hall. Maybe we hustle to get the validation we need from our boss because our father shamed us. Perhaps we hustle to gain someone's attention we think we need or desire for them to tell us we're good enough. We may hustle to show the world that we have it all together and didn't come from dysfunction. We hustle for compliments or hustle to make our children's lives better than what we experienced. My dear friends, there is no freedom in the hustle.

I did the hustle. I avoided memories on the surface. But internally, I characterized myself as a victim, almost like wearing a badge of honor. Part of me didn't believe anyone could understand my pain. On some level, no one else having the same experiences made me feel like my story was special. Holding onto my unique story made it easier to blame others for their lack of understanding. There was no victory or freedom. Instead of validating sin as sin, I justified it. Without realizing it, sin became my identity.

The nomination

Entering the Hall of Shame may be something we are reluctant to do because sin isn't pretty and it isn't glamourous. If we've sinned or been sinned against, we're in. If we sin in response to sin, we're in. No nominations. No gold stars. No celebrations.

In this hall, you'll see the faces of shame, which can sneak into every corner of your lives. Shame may show up as a lack of confidence, anger, self-righteousness, feelings of inadequacy, or reluctance to try new things. Shame shows up as failure to reach your potential. Shame blames others or circumstances for lack of success. Shame believes *you* are bad, instead of sin being bad, because shame doesn't separate the person from the action. By directly tying our actions to our essence, we forget about our divine space. Instead, we get embarrassed by pain, and develop self-destructive strategies, like addictions. Shame can lead to anxiety, depression, or numbing ourselves with drugs, alcohol, or sex. So why enter the Hall?

To be known

I think we can all admit that shame doesn't feel good. But to know ourselves and to be known, we have to acknowledge not only the good things we are, but we must validate sin for what it is. Ultimately, we cannot receive healing until we acknowledge we need it. The good news is that once sin is acknowledged, it ceases to have power over us.

So, go ahead and enter the hall, but don't plan to stay there. The goal is to enter the Hall, identify and name the sin and our response to it, acknowledge its effect on our life, and then move on.

As a lay counselor, I've heard a number of clients avoid the shame they felt when being bullied as a child. Most of them were scared to tell anyone or were not believed when they told their teacher or parents. Some adults may have dismissed it as "just kids being kids." What if your bullying was never acknowledged as bullying? *Enter the Hall.*

What if you were sexually abused as a child? Did you tell anyone? Did they believe you? It is common for sexual abuse victims to repress memories. I believe it is God's beautiful way of protecting the child until they are ready to face it. In the meantime, if no one listens, what do we do? *Enter the Hall.*

Chapter 8 – Enter the Hall

What if you have a porn addiction and feel terrible about it? What if no one knew but you? What if your spouse has the problem? Are you embarrassed? *Enter the Hall.*

Friends, God wants you to visit the Hall for healing, but remember, it's just a visit. It's Satan who encourages us to stay. He wants us to ruminate on sins to justify our self-righteousness and keep us pre-occupied. He wants us to hide because when we expose sin, we expose him.

Another hall

When we name sin for what it is, we are working through our salvation, not working for it. Paul describes this in Philippians 2:12: *"Therefore, my beloved, as you have always obeyed, so now, not only as in my presence, but now even more in my absence, work out your salvation with fear and trembling."*

My dear readers, sin is what Jesus came to save us from! Sin is the spiritual battle we talk about, the fight of our lives! Removal of shame can be satisfied only when darkness is brought to light. Eventually, everything will be exposed. Luke 8:17 tells us, *"For nothing is hidden that will not be made manifest, nor is anything secret that will not be known and come to light."*

What happens when we bring sin to the light? We expose the enemy and attack shame at the source. We acknowledge it but it doesn't mean we affirm it. By naming it, we can claim it, and position ourselves to receive the mercy of Jesus. We look to Jesus as our source of salvation instead of expecting others to compensate for sin. But only if we don't respond to sin with sin.

Our visit to Hall of Shame extends when we end up sinning in response to sin. This happens when we get bitter, fail to forgive, or feel justified. This tactic the enemy uses to keep you burying in shame or self-righteousness. Sometimes, he even uses sin committed against as a means to seek out excess approval. There is no freedom in the search.

As you experience the freedom only Jesus brings, we get to look forward to a huge celebration at the feast of the Lamb. It starts by looking to the cross. When we do, what happens? Psalms 34:5 (NIV) tells us, *"Those who look to him are radiant; their faces are never covered with shame."*

Enter the Hall to acknowledge the sin, and your sinful response to sin. But as you leave the hall, God will replace shame with mercy, allowing your facet to shine. Radiance awaits.

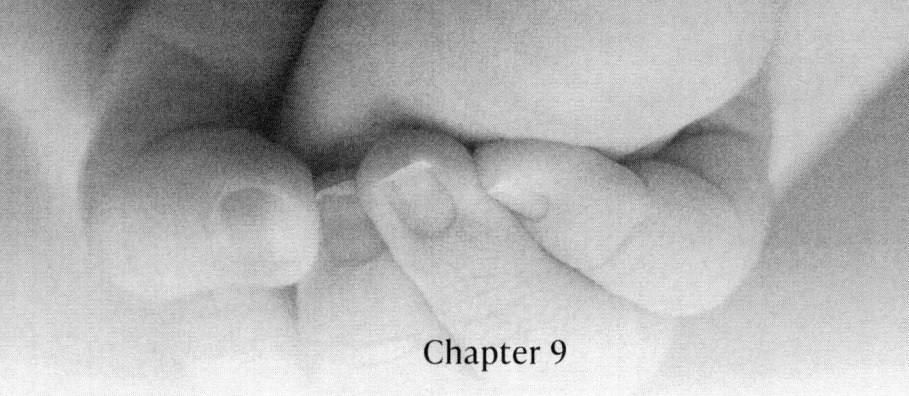

Chapter 9

THE VOW

———————— " ————————

A tree that is unbending is easily broken.
—**Lao Tzu**

*"Again, you have heard that it was said to those of
old, 'You shall not swear falsely, but shall perform to
the Lord what you have sworn.' But I say to you,
Do not take an oath at all, either by heaven, for
it is the throne of God, or by the earth, for it is his
footstool, or by Jerusalem, for it is the city of the
great King. And do not take an oath by your head,
for you cannot make one hair white or black.
Let what you say be simply 'Yes' or 'No';
anything more than this comes from evil."*
—**Matthew 5:33-37**

Green leather booths lined the VA hospital's waiting room. Nearby racks provided magazines, coloring books, and crayons while I watched my three brothers squirm in the corner. Sometimes, cousins would stop by, or nurses would play with us, but most of the time we had to occupy ourselves while Mom visited Dad. On one particular day, we arrived after school at about 4:00 p.m. Relief came four and a half hours later when visiting hours were over. This childhood scene became all too familiar.

Plagued by rheumatic fever as a child, Dad had severe heart problems, including having his first heart attack at age twenty-six. He also had Berger's disease, which resulted in one of his legs being amputated above the knee and the other below the knee. Although I barely remember him walking with his wooden leg, this was before handicapped accessibility or prosthetics, so getting around wasn't easy. The wheelchair became his primary mode of transportation.

Being in and out of the hospital prevented Dad from holding down a job, so finances were a problem. Hand-me-downs, subsidized summer camps, and food stamps were commonplace. Dad instilled in us a strong work ethic. Not only was work his identity, he believed a man, especially a Polish Catholic man, must provide for his wife and family. Reality framed it differently.

When a man from our church who owned a local TV shop offered to teach Dad how to repair TVs, he jumped at the chance. Working from home appealed to him. Work made him feel useful and being at home kept looks from strangers to a minimum. I fondly remember him hobbling down the basement steps one by one on his bottom. He beamed with pride to be able to contribute to the family income. Although Mom and Dad appeared to get along well, it was money which caused arguments.

Mom kept insisting on getting a job, but Dad said no. I overheard this argument multiple times before Dad finally conceded. Mom took a job as a school secretary for the Catholic school attached to our church. Her small church salary only went so far.

Not having money was challenging for Mom. She loved crafts. Whatever was the lastest craft, she did. When I was ten, a few days

Chapter 9 – The Vow

before Valentine's Day, she encouraged me to make my Dad a card. I was proud of the red and pink hearts I drew and how I colored his name on it. I was so excited about my creation I begged Mom to let me give it to him early. She finally caved in. So three days before Valentine's Day, I gave him the card. He was not only excited about it but seemed to be very grateful for it. This was probably the only time I can remember feeling validated and affirmed by him.

Ironically, giving him that card early turned out to be an extraordinary memory. Days later, on Valentine's Day, Dad passed away from a heart attack at forty years old. Mom was thirty-six, I was ten, and my brothers were twelve, thirteen, and fourteen.

The vow

Grief showed up differently for all of us. Most of our concerns were financial, all of us carrying the burden of finding additional sources of income. Babysitting, paper routes, mowing lawns, or working under the table became ways to earn money. Work, school, and extra-curriculars kept my brothers busy, so I spent most of my time with Mom. She didn't have great coping skills, and day after day, I could tell she wasn't okay. The look of stress in her eyes as she adapted to life as a single mom was apparent. Financial pressure consumed her, but the biggest concern for her was not being home after school. Unsupervised teenage boys caused a myriad of problems.

The stress and anxiety she experienced, combined with a lack of inadequate life skills, made everything about survival. Rarely recalling fun memories, I know she tried. Her struggles and the unhealthy way she took out her frustrations left me determined. I never wanted to be in her situation.

So, I made a vow. I told myself, "I will go to college and be able to financially support myself in case anything ever happened to my husband."

This was an internal vow. It was one I've never shared with anyone. However, I said it out loud to myself many times because it was fuel for my choices. Decisions made from that point on were directly related to that vow. Even big decisions, including which college I attended, who I married, what job I took, or what opportunities I dismissed, were viewed through the lens of that vow. I wanted to protect myself since no one seemed to protect or provide for me. And I certainly didn't want to live my Mom's life.

Internal vows are those promises we make to perform some act or live in a certain way. Typically, an adverse event is the motivation. As a response, we make a vow we think may protect us, correct a wrong, or preserve our self-esteem. For example, my husband's father struggled with drinking, so my husband vowed never to drink, never to lose control. In my case, I made this vow to protect myself and to help right the injustice I saw. I lived this vow without even realizing it.

In the book *Captivating* by Stasi Eldredge, she discusses a vow she made: "And so I made a vow. Somewhere in my young heart, without even knowing I was doing it or putting words to it, I vowed to protect myself by never causing pain, never requiring attention. My job in the family was to be invisible, to cause no waves. If I upset things at all, surely this ship would sink. So, I began to hide. I hid my needs, my desires, my very heart. I hid my true self. And when it was all too much, I hid in the closet...The vows we make as children are very understandable—and very, very damaging. They shut our hearts down. They are essentially a deep-seated agreement with the message of the wounds. They act as an agreement with the verdict on us."

The effect

Vows can manifest in different ways. First, the vow denounces the message by trying to prove the person who said it was wrong. As we look to others to affirm our perspective, we may come across as defensive or self-righteous. Second, we agree with the message. This agreement tells us something is wrong with us. When we feel something is wrong with us, we will seek more validation and affirmation.

I recall the story of an intelligent young man who ended up graduating from high school with a 1.5 GPA. Most teachers didn't have much hope for his future. In fact, one of them said "You're a loser. The only thing you'll end up doing is pumping gas." Wounded, he didn't want to believe the message. So, he made a vow to prove the teacher wrong. He was determined to make something of his life, and he did.

Another young man overheard a conversation between his mom and a neighborhood friend. "He's not going to amount to anything" was what he heard. For the majority of his life, he believed these words were said about him. Believing this message, he lived thinking whatever he did wouldn't measure up to his brothers. This message altered his relationship with his mom, his siblings and himself. Once he believed that message was about him, he viewed every exchange with her through the eyes of that one statement. Ironically, shortly before his mom died, he discovered the comment wasn't made about him at all.

A vow made for self-protection can promote reliance on self, rather than reliance on God. Believing you have special powers to change things may encourage self-righteousness. On the other hand, a vow based on misperceptions makes it difficult for us to recognize someone else's facets. All we're left with is the feeling that we don't measure up. So we choose to do something, anything, to get rid of that feeling.

How have vows been your fuel, your motivator? Were they made to protect yourself or prove something? Have you been able to fulfill them?

What God says about vows

God takes vows seriously. Deuteronomy 23:21-23 explains: *"If you make a vow to the LORD your God, you shall not delay fulfilling it, for the LORD your God will surely require it of you, and you will be guilty of sin. But if you refrain from vowing, you will not be guilty of sin. You shall be careful to do what has passed your lips, for you have voluntarily vowed to the LORD your God what you have promised with your mouth."*

In the Old Testament, especially the book of Judges, we learn about vows. Vows made with people, animals, houses, and inheritances were mostly a vow made with God. Without legal documents to hold men accountable, what you said you were going to do was binding. So naturally, when people broke a vow, it was a bad thing. However, could you make a bad vow? Yes. One biblical example is Jephthah, a judge in Israel. The story is told in Judges 11:29-31, which says:

> *Then the Spirit of the Lord came upon Jephthah, and he passed over Gilead, and Manasseh, and passed over Mizpeh of Gilead, and from Mizpeh of Gilead he passed over unto the children of Ammon. And Jephthah vowed a vow unto the Lord, and said, If thou shalt without fail deliver the children of Ammon into mine hands, then it shall be, that whatsoever cometh forth of the doors of my house to meet me, when I return in peace from the children of Ammon, shall surely be the Lord's, and I will offer it up for a burnt offering.*

A few issues surfaced. Jephthah should not have made this vow. We know the Bible condemns human sacrifice. Not only that, imagine his surprise when it turned out to be his daughter who came forth to meet him at the door. To fulfill his vow, Jephthah would have to offer her up as a burnt offering!

Perhaps we have not made a vow with such dire consequences. However, the fruit from inner vows can lie dormant for years and manifest itself outwardly through anger, guilt, anxiety, or excessive need for affirmation. Unfulfilled vows can leave us feeling shame. Vows achieved may cause us to be prideful. A sense of inadequacy or false confidence can result.

In the New Testament, Jesus shares with us the Parable of the Two Sons in Matthew 21:28-31.

> *What do you think? A man had two sons. Now he came to the first and said, "Son, go and work in the vineyard today." "No, I don't want to," he replied. But later, he changed his mind and went. The father said the same thing to the other son, who replied, "Yes, sir." But he didn't go. Which one of these two did his father's will? They said, "The first one."*

This story seems to identify that what we do holds more credibility than what we say we're going to do. Jesus confirms this in Matthew 5:37: *"Let what you say be simply 'Yes' or 'No'; anything more than this comes from evil."*

So, if you have made a vow from an immature vantage point fueled by a negative experience to protect yourself, isn't God saying He has a better way?

Grasping mercy

Vows grounded in judgment may be rooted in fear. Replacing fear with trust in God encourages confidence in God instead of self. How do we know we can trust Him? Because God is merciful, just, and will repay evil for evil. By having a firm grasp of mercy, we'll be able to give it away. Could a first step be offering mercy to the individual that initiated your vow?

Mercy has many facets. Mercy considers the possibility that you don't know what you don't know. Perhaps the person was experiencing stress, had wounds from their past, or was blinded by their sin. Maybe they weren't even talking about you.

Mercy provides a landing place for failures. We all have limits, make mistakes, and sin. We sin in response to sin.

Mercy understands that all of us need help. We can't do it alone. Vows are about trying to solve problems on our own. If you've made a vow, rescind it. If you didn't fulfill your vow, resist punishing yourself or needing affirmation to prove your vow was justified. Confess. Repent. Cleanse. Receive.

The young man proved his teacher wrong. Even years later, he talks of how he successfully fulfilled that vow. Still, I wonder if the teacher ever remembered saying it. This young man determined his destiny by someone who probably doesn't remember his name. Ironically, the way the other boy lived out his vow held him back. For years, he lived believing a lie about himself and didn't give his mom the benefit of the doubt. Excessive affirmation becomes needed to counterbalance negative vows.

How have you responded to your wounds? Did you make a vow? Have you cramped your potential by living in shame and resentment? James 5:12 says it all: *"Now above all, my brothers, do not swear, either by heaven or by earth or with any other oath. Your 'yes' must be 'yes,' and your 'no' must be 'no,' so that you won't fall under judgment."*

As you get a firm grasp, you'll release your vows and begin to live a life of mercy. Mercy triumphs over judgment.

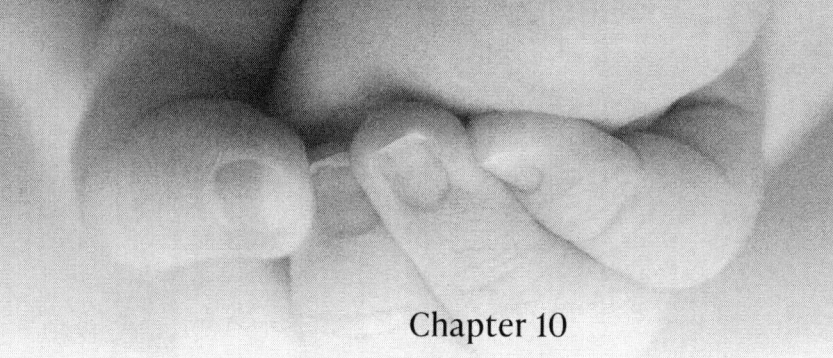

Chapter 10

THE TRAP

—— " ——

When you are willing to do what you're not qualified to do, sometimes, that's what qualifies you.
—Bill Johnson

The trouble was, I had been inadequate all along, I simply hadn't thought about it.
—Sylvia Plath

My heart skipped a few beats as I took the necessary steps towards the microphone. The room was full of over two-hundred women, somewhat apprehensive to hear sexual abuse testimonies. Although victory in Jesus was the glorious anthem for this event, it was the first time I shared my personal story in a public setting. What was I feeling? In a word: inadequate.

Although some of us are more comfortable speaking in public than others, nervousness happens. As a professional musician, I've experienced the usual symptoms before a performance—quick, uneasy breathing, loss of focus, hyper-focused attention to detail, and inability to complete a sentence. After years of experience, I've grown accustomed to knowing when it's coming, and I plan for it. The feeling usually goes away when I take a deep breath and warm up on my instrument. At that moment, I remind myself that yes, I can play. After each note resonates, and I can feel myself breathing, I slowly change my mindset. Then I pray. More times than not, it's not just nervousness. Deep down, at the root of it all, is a feeling of inadequacy.

The battlefield

Life experiences create an environment of anxiousness and fear, leading us to doubt our capabilities. At times, we *feel* inadequate. At times, we *are* inadequate. Perhaps our family's focus was on accomplishments, defining success by high points on the basketball court or an all "A" report card. Maybe we attempted something new only to experience failure.

In the battlefield of the mind, the feelings of inadequacies we had as children may surface in adult life. Vacillating between low self-esteem and ego, failure and success, or being celebrated or unnoticed, we are left living in extremes. This shows up when we judge others or set ourselves up for impossible standards we can't meet. As we view ourselves through our own eyes and come up short, we are sometimes left fearful, paralyzed, and ineffective. We don't know whose standards to live by. In our minds, we're just inadequate. It's the trap.

Timothy Keller, in his book *The Freedom of Self-Forgetfulness* states: "What would Paul say to those who tell him to set his own standards? He would say it is a trap. A trap he will not fall into. You see, it is a trap to say that we should not worry about everyone else's standards, just set our own. That's not an answer. Boosting our self-esteem by living up to our own standards or someone else's sounds like a great solution. But it does not deliver. It cannot deliver.

I cannot live up to my parents' standards—and that makes me feel terrible. I cannot live up to your standards—and that makes me feel terrible. I cannot live up to society's standards—and that makes me feel terrible. I cannot live up to other societies' standards—and that makes me feel terrible. Perhaps the solution is to set my own standards? But I cannot keep them either—and that makes me feel terrible, unless I set up incredibly low standards. Are low standards a solution? Not at all. That makes me feel terrible because I realize I am the type of person who has low standards. Trying to boost our self-esteem by trying to live up to our own standards or someone else's is a trap. It's not the answer."

Ironically, we are not alone when it comes to the trap of inadequacy. Many Old Testament saints got caught in the trap. Moses, Jeremiah, Gideon, and Isaiah are great examples.

We are not alone

God told Moses to lead the Israelites out of Egypt, but Moses didn't feel up to the assignment. His response in Exodus 3:11 says it all: *"But Moses said to God, 'Who am I that I should go to Pharaoh and bring the children of Israel out of Egypt?'"* Exodus 4:10 and 13 amplified the concept: *"But Moses said to the LORD, 'Oh, my Lord, I am not eloquent, either in the past or since you have spoken to your servant, but I am slow of speech and of tongue.'"* In verse 13, he continues, *"Oh, my Lord, please send someone else."*

Let's analyze Moses for a minute. Something happened to Moses in childhood. One might suggest Moses had problems with his identity. After all, he was born an Israelite, but raised in an Egyptian family. Wouldn't it be easy for him to get in the trap basing his identity on what he did since he wasn't sure who he was? Moses' upbringing taught him the Israelites would be free from slavery, but he wasn't aware of what role he would play.

There's more. Moses messed up big time. Later, when he found out he was an Israelite, he saw an Egyptian abusing an Israelite and killed him. When the pharaoh sought to execute him, Moses ran into exile for forty years! Sin definitely makes us feel inadequate, shameful even. Ironically, even after forty years, Moses still dwelled on his inadequacies.

Jeremiah was born into a religious home. His father was a priest. In today's terms, he would be the equivalent of a PK (pastor's kid), his training and background grooming him for a life of service. However, Jeremiah did not become a priest. He did not follow in his father's footsteps. Instead, Jeremiah became a prophet, a non-paid vocation. One could speculate that Jeremiah felt inadequate because he didn't carry on the tradition of his family. In other words, his fan club might be deficient. Yet God told him in Jeremiah 1:5, *"Before I formed you in the womb, I knew you and before you were born, I consecrated you; I appointed you a prophet to the nations."* Even though the Lord God came right out and told him this, Jeremiah still felt inadequate. Jeremiah 1:6 states: *"Then I said, 'Ah, Lord GOD! Behold, I do not know how to speak, for I am only a youth.'"*

"Holy, holy, holy, Lord God Almighty" rang true for Isaiah. As a prophet, he had a vision from God where he saw angels and the almighty God Himself high and lifted up. His first reaction in Isaiah 6:5 revealed his response: *"And I said: 'Woe is me! For I am lost; for I am a man of unclean lips, and I dwell in the midst of a people of unclean lips; for my eyes have seen the King, the LORD of hosts!'"* Friends, Isaiah saw God! Yes, I think we would all agree that seeing God would humble any of us, but would we characterize that as a "woe is me" moment?

What about Gideon? Gideon felt so negatively about himself that when God first called him, he didn't believe God could possibly be speaking to him. We could say in today's terms, he was insecure.

Needing a sign, he laid out a fleece—not once, but twice—to test the waters. Even when God gave him a sign, he was not convinced. Eventually, he went ahead and did what God asked of Him. But along the way, he was hopelessly unsure. He didn't have a firm grasp.

Dependence

Let's take a look at a different story in the Old Testament about King Jehoshaphat. This story depicts a different mindset about challenges. As the war approached, King Jehoshaphat began to feel nervous and inadequate. As he became self-aware of his inadequacies, he ***acknowledged*** them. Here's the clue: He admitted he needed God. 2 Chronicles 20:12 tells us, *"O our God, will you not execute judgment on them? For we are powerless against this great horde that is coming against us. We do not know what to do, **but our eyes are on you.**"*

Dependency on God IS the root of humility. Humility acknowledges inadequacies, prompting us to reach out to God. What's even better is when humility embraces mercy. Our inadequacies are no longer an issue. Dependence on God is.

How would the lives of these saints be changed if they started out depending on God? What if we, too, could accept that we will not receive punishment for our inadequacies? Is the trap of inadequacy keeping us from the call?

I understand we all feel inadequate sometimes. It's part of being human. We have limits and make mistakes. Just ask me anytime I need a handyman. I get started on a project thinking I can handle it, only to become overwhelmed with how much I don't know. None of us are going to stop doing projects or setting goals because we have limitations. Instead, because we are limited, we ask for help. Validation acknowledges our limits. And it's okay!

However, sometimes in the name of humility, we focus on limitations way too much. We become self-effacing, criticizing, or putting ourselves down, answering the wrong call. Instead of listening to God's call, we become like Gideon—insecure. Friends, you know what this leads to. Please, someone, make me feel better about myself. Tell me I'm wonderful instead. This kind of self-effacement can beckon more attention by turning the focus to self.

With humility as the goal, Louis Giglio says in *Waiting Here*, "Humility is not thinking you are less; it is never forgetting the fact that it is Jesus who made you more." Continual emphasis on our inadequacies may reveal we are thinking more about ourselves than we need to.

So how do we divert attention back to God? Let's go back to our Old Testament friends. Yes, they felt inadequate, but God was still there, teaching them to remember, persist, obey and acknowledge.

Remember

Remember God told Moses in Exodus 5:4, *"I am who I say I am."* He was very clear what he wanted Moses to say to the Israelites: *"**I AM** has sent me to you."* Did God try to make Moses feel better or try to prop him up? I don't see that in the passage. Instead, God was encouraging Moses to focus on **who** sent him. **I AM**.

Friends, when someone talks about their inadequacies, be careful. If we immediately express empathy or use words of affirmation in the name of support, we may be trying to rescue someone from the conviction of God. Perhaps instead of saying "you got this"; we encourage language which supports dependence on God. God's response to Moses implies his inadequacies were irrelevant. Remember WHO sent you!

Persist

How would you feel if you sent a message over and over, and no one listened? Jeremiah kept sending the message, but the people ignored it. Perhaps Jeremiah thought there was something he was doing wrong since results weren't coming. He probably started problem solving and might have asked questions like: Should I say it differently? Did I not use the right inflections?

Sometimes, we have to *persist* in sending the message even if it feels like it's falling on deaf ears. Humanly speaking, we understand why Jeremiah grew weary. But remember, it wasn't Jeremiah who was rejected. It was the message. In Jeremiah 20:9, he said, *"If I say, 'I will not mention him, or speak any more in his name,' there is in my heart as it were a burning fire shut up in my bones, and I am weary with holding it in, and I cannot."* God put this message into his very bones, so he had to persist. Without God's help, he struggled. With God's help, he persisted.

Obey

Gideon tried all kinds of end runs. Perhaps his insecurities were a lack of trust in God. Eventually, after waiting for many signs, he took action and obeyed. Because of his obedience, you can see how God equipped him to eventually become a confident and courageous leader.

In Judges 7:17-18, this confidence is reflected when Gideon says, *"And he said to them, 'Look at me, and do likewise. When I come to the outskirts of the camp, do as I do. When I blow the trumpet, I and all who are with me, then blow the trumpets also on every side of all the camp and shout, "For the LORD and for Gideon."'"*

What's the best way to combat inadequacy? Confidence. How did Gideon become confident? Obedience.

Acknowledge

Isaiah. Although it may appear that Isaiah felt inadequate, one might conclude that Isaiah became humbled at the sight of God. He knew what it was like to be in God's presence, and acknowledged he wasn't God. God answered through a dream. The dream addressed the root of the problem of inadequacy: sin.

Isaiah 6:6-7 tells us, *"Then one of the seraphim flew to me, having in his hand a burning coal that he had taken with tongs from the altar. And he touched my mouth and said: 'Behold, this has touched your lips; your guilt is taken away, and your sin atoned for.'"*

Acknowledging our sin is humility. Dwelling on it isn't.

The source

What makes you feel inadequate? Is it when you try something and fail? Or when you compare yourself? Do you blame your childhood, weaknesses, or lack of capabilities? Or your inadequate fan club?

Friends, this may seem a little harsh, but it's the truth. We need to get used to living with the discomfort of feeling inadequate, because we are. As we've discussed in other chapters, we have limits, we make mistakes, and we sin. Sin makes us feel inadequate. Sin makes us feel like a failure. Sin makes us feel like we don't measure up. And shouldn't it?

Instead of being aware and accepting our limitations, mistakes, and sin, we want someone, anyone, to make us feel better. Could that be why we'd rather have the preacher tell us how much God loves us instead of how much He hates sin? But here's the great hope: when we accept Christ, our inadequacies aren't an issue to God any longer!

There's more. We can replace our feelings of inadequacy with a straightforward message: mercy. Our Savior removed our iniquity

Chapter 10 – The Trap

through His atonement, allowing mercy to touch our lips. Don't let the enemy trap you!

May we relinquish our feelings of inadequacy and respond as Isaiah did in Isaiah 6:8-9: *"And I heard the voice of the Lord saying, 'Whom shall I send, and who will go for us?' Then I said, 'Here I am! Send me.'"*

Our friends in the Old Testament, with all their inadequacies, inevitably became role models. No, they didn't always get it right. But just like us, they learned to acknowledge their inadequacies and eventually obeyed, persisted, and remembered who sent them, allowing them to fulfill the mission.

We are on mission too.

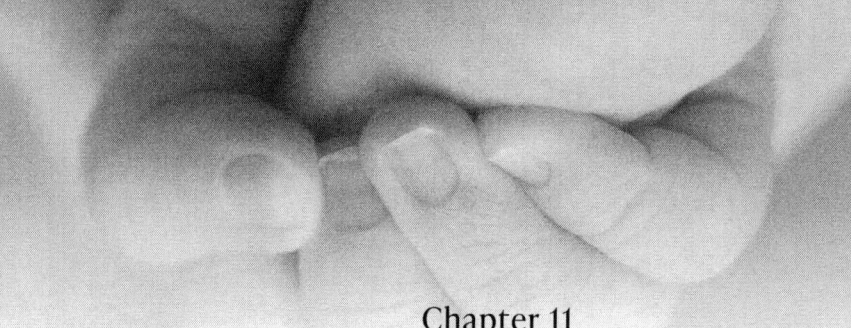

Chapter 11

CRAMPS

Sometimes, I find myself in the eye of my own hurricane...
—**Melody Lee, Vine: Book of Poetry**

Resentment is like drinking poison and waiting for the other person to die.
—**Saint Augustine**

Running. Not my favorite activity, but something I started to lower my blood pressure. My husband, who is a runner, encouraged me to run some 5ks. For those of you who are actual runners, 5ks may seem lame, but running is arduous work for me. Even when I was in my early twenties and in my best shape ever, I struggled to run close to an eight-minute mile. For me to attempt, let alone finish, a 5k, well, it's a big deal.

Still, I wouldn't say I like running. Although my 5k times were inconsistent, I continued to run because I enjoyed how I felt afterward. Until that day. I was running on a circular trail around a pond at a nearby college campus. A sudden, extremely sharp pain in my calf stopped me in my tracks. Ouch! A cramp worse than birth contractions. Although the pain didn't last long, I couldn't continue running. It hurt. I was stalled.

Respond-ability

Physical cramps come out of nowhere. So can other kinds of cramps. Psychologists call them triggers. We may be on mission, running the race, when a cramp comes out of nowhere. The cramp might attack as health problems, financial loss, relational difficulties, or a trigger from our frame. Whatever the enemy knows will cramp our work for the kingdom, he will do. He wants to thwart God's message any way he can.

When these cramps come, how do we respond? What do we do when sin in our life exposes itself to the light? Do we respond to sin *with* sin?

This is where "respond-ability" comes in. In its simplest form, respond-ability is a word I created to explain our responsibility for our response. Respond-ability recognizes the free will we have to choose our response to those cramps.

C-R-A-M-P-S

Cleverly disguised, cramps can render us powerless—if we let them. Some say life is ten percent what happens to you and ninety percent how you respond. But what about that ten percent? Aren't we still one hundred percent responsible for that ten percent?

Using CRAMPS as an acronym, let's take a look at different ways we may respond to sin. Though these responses may appear to the world to be justified, they don't reflect the fruits of the Spirit. The first three—catastrophe, resentment, and approbation—are

Chapter 11 – Cramps

responses most people would characterize as "sinful" responses. The other three—manipulation, performance, and striving—are responses that appear clever or good but are part of our sin nature's "human-good" side.

Spending time being still is a great way to connect with God and process the way we respond to sin. Ask Him. The goal is self-awareness. Maybe you don't respond in these destructive ways, but you recognize it in others. Hurt people—hurt people. The more we understand hurt, the more we can be merciful.

C–CATASTROPHE

Catastrophes are creative embellishments or wild imaginings. It's sort of like a negative fish story where you embellish, embellish, embellish. Often, this may start out as a complaint, but then we find ourselves getting overly upset and then turn it into a soap opera scene. We may respond by drawing a conclusion about someone or something that isn't warranted by the symptoms. Sometimes, our loved ones experience our catastrophes when we project our feelings of powerlessness over another incident onto them.

For example, let's say the waiter forgets to refill your water. You're thirsty, and you see him busy chatting with the next table. Really? He isn't acknowledging you. He doesn't notice you. How do you respond?

What if another driver cuts you off in traffic? Do you immediately call them a jerk or create some kind of story in your head about why they did what they did? Or worse yet, do you create a reason they would do that to *you*?

What if your boss has different political views from yours? Do you respond by maligning or gossiping about him to others?

If you respond to cramps by creating a catastrophe, you may find that your story becomes a drama. Instead of "he raised his voice," it somehow escalates to "he was screaming and yelling at me so loud the neighbors heard." If our minds turn to wild imaginations and we use dramatic voice to tell our story, what are we seeking?

In the story of David and Goliath, David is portrayed as the star, but he didn't start that way. When David brought up the idea of fighting Goliath, he wasn't validated. First, his dad didn't even tell Samuel, the prophet about him. His brothers brought up his inadequacies, and Saul questioned him. What might it have looked like if David had turned this into a catastrophe?

His response could have been to dwell on the trap of inadequacy or call his brother's facet slanderous. He could have taken things personally when Saul questioned him or wondered what happened to his fan club. Maybe he could make a vow to never do anything for anyone if they weren't affirming him.

Catastrophes may be our response of choice because we need others to validate or affirm us. We may create catastrophes because we're responding to previous injustices or a need to be heard. Maybe, in our pride, we point out the other's wrong so we can be right. Only you and God can know your motives. Any way you look at it, catastrophes send us off track and often turn into gossip or bearing false witness. Bearing false witness is one of the Ten Commandments!

Could the enemy be trying to cramp David's focus? David chose not to dwell on his deficient fan club, inadequacies, or the facets of others. Instead, He stayed focused on the mission and what God had called him to do.

Like David, we need to discern whether something is a big deal or not. Could we be turning something into a Goliath-sized problem when it isn't? Proverbs 16:32 warns, *"Whoever is slow to anger is better than the mighty, and he who rules his spirit than he who takes a city."*

R–RESENTMENT

Resentment is the feeling of displeasure we receive from an injury or insult. Responding to life's events with resentment is usually triggered because of unfair treatment, either real or imagined. We usually don't think of resentment's gateway as envy, but it can be. We may become envious when others get the validation or affirmation we crave, or defensive because someone doesn't see us the way we see ourselves. It's just another strategy the enemy uses.

One of the most well-known stories in the Bible is the tale of Cain and Abel. Cain started out envious of Abel's relationship with God and determined that God was unfair. Envy turned to resentment, which often presents itself as bitterness. The first cramp Cain felt was envy. He wanted what Abel had with God. Cain damns God and kills his brother. It all started by not feeling noticed.

Although we may not allow the situation to escalate to murder, the roots of resentment and bitterness are ugly. Perhaps we don't feel like it's a cramp because unfairness needs to be justified.

We may target other people, but just like Cain, resentment is more likely to be about our relationship with God. Take a look at the way Naomi responded in Ruth 1:19-21 when she thought God was being unfair to her:

> *So the two of them went on until they came to Bethlehem. And when they came to Bethlehem, the whole town was stirred because of them. And the women said, "Is this Naomi?" She said to them, "Do not call me Naomi; call me Mara, for the Almighty has dealt very bitterly with me. I went away full, and the Lord has brought me back empty. Why call me Naomi, when the Lord has testified against me and the Almighty has brought calamity upon me?"*

Naomi (Mara) resented God because she saw how God seemed to provide for others but didn't provide for her. It started with envy and turned into resentment. She even changed her name!

We may not be aware of our resentment towards God, because we are told to respect Him. We don't easily express negative feelings about God to God. That may be a reason we deflect to another person. Perhaps the person who sinned against you didn't receive any punishment, so you tried to determine their punishment. Maybe you come up with solutions without asking God for help. Unforgiveness does not seek God.

Job 36:13 (NLT) tells us, *"For the godless are full of resentment; Even when he punishes them, they refuse to cry out to him for help."* Ephesians 4:31 says, *"Let all bitterness and wrath and anger and clamor and slander be put away from you, along with all malice."*

A—APPROBATION

Approbation is a fancy word for the lust for praise or for attention. Sometimes when we've been sinned against, we want comfort. We seek someone to validate we are right, agree with our position, and claim the person who sinned against us is wrong. If that isn't satisfied, we cling to anyone who sees things from the same perspective we do. If we don't change our response, the enemy uses this as a way to cramp the mission. By taking things personally, we make it about us, not the other person, and certainly, not about God. We may choose self-indulgence—like eating too much, drinking, or sex—to numb these feelings.

As we've learned, wanting the praise of men isn't something new. Lucifer wanted it, and because we are created for relationship, we need it too. Sometimes people pleasing can help us get the approbation we desire. A biblical example of those who lusted after approbation were the Pharisees. John 12:42-43 discusses how approbation fails us:

> *Nevertheless, many even of the authorities believed in him, but for fear of the Pharisees they did not confess it, so that they would not be put out of the synagogue; for they loved the glory that comes from man more than the glory that comes from God.*

From the book, *Love's Greatest Challenges*, John Ritenbaugh writes more about the Pharisees. "These men feared that, if they committed themselves to love God, they would lose the approbation of their religious peers. If they stepped out, they would lose what they already had. So, it kept them from loving God, and of course, it kept them from loving man too because God would have given them growth if they had continued yielding to Him."

The enemy cramps again. Why? To thwart the message.

M–MANIPULATION

To manipulate is to negotiate, control, or influence, strictly for one's advantage, or to change someone's mind. Subtle and skillful, a manipulator is often charming and enticing with words. Encouraging one another by affirming them through words is a good thing. But the enemy cramps the true message when encouragement is couched in flattery or guilt.

Suppose you need to persuade someone to your way of thinking. Have you considered they may be looking at a different facet of the situation? Do you need to change their perspective, or do you need to accept them where they are? We need to be careful not to offer validation and affirmation to someone just so they will give it back.

The story of Samson and Delilah is a biblical example of manipulation. Delilah was crafty, using guilt and charm as her weapon so Samson would tell her the secret to his strength. Be cautious in dealing with manipulative people and be careful not to use it yourself. Don't give others what is sacred. This is another one of the enemy's clever tactics to cramp the mission. Matthew 7:6 warns us, *"Do not give dogs what is holy, and do not throw your pearls before pigs, lest they trample them underfoot and turn to attack you."*

P–PERFORMANCE

The enemy cramps our ability to stay on mission through performance. Hypocrisy translates from the Greek as "actor." Like an actor, performance is when we pretend in order to keep up appearances.

Although God sees all, there is a part of our sin nature that wants to "cover up" or make sure we appear a certain way to others. This level of acting can fill us with anxiety. Impostor syndrome is a psychological pattern in which an individual doubts their skills, talents or accomplishments and have a persistent internalized fear of being exposed as a fraud. Internally, we may feel like a fraud, but on the outside, we give a great performance. That is another tactic of the enemy.

2 Corinthians 11:14-15 says, *"And no wonder, for even Satan disguises himself as an angel of light. So, it is no surprise if his servants, also, disguise themselves as servants of righteousness. Their end will correspond to their deeds."* Keep in mind that pretense will eventually be revealed.

In Luke 12:2, we read, *"Nothing is covered up that will not be revealed or hidden that will not be known."*

S–STRIVING

Do you ever feel like you're the only one who can solve a problem? Or do you go to extreme lengths to avoid a problem? As we discussed in a previous chapter, hypervigilance is the state of being abnormally alert to potential danger or threat, allowing you to make sure you've covered all your bases. This kind of striving is based on fear but can be disguised as perfectionism. Others may call it controlling.

For example, let's say you have guests over, and you want to ensure that everything is set up just right. No one would fault someone for doing that, but what's the motivation? Are you concerned your guests will question your housekeeping abilities? Are you hoping they will affirm you about your lovely home? Or is your desire to make your guests comfortable and treat them well?

A biblical example of striving would be Martha. Though she was not wrong for serving her guests, she appeared more concerned about being acknowledged by the Lord for working hard while her sister did "nothing." She wanted him to take notice.

Deliverance

Catastrophes, resentment, approbation, manipulation, performance, and striving are just six ways the enemy tries to cramp us. Which one challenges you the most? Are you more aware of the deceptive way the enemy tries to make you believe you are doing good, even though you are actually trying to win others' favor?

Looking back at the David and Goliath story, one could think David was the star, but he wasn't. God was. Yet later in life, David sinned big time. He turned his sin into a catastrophe. After he committed adultery with Bathsheba and she became pregnant, he tried to make Bathsheba's husband sleep with her to cover up his sin. When that didn't work, he ended up having her husband murdered in battle.

And then he went into a literal hiding place as his enemies sought after him. In essence, he responded to sin with sin—catastrophically.

David went from sitting on the throne, to hiding in the desert, parched, and full of shame. He was no longer a star. What happened to his fan club? Caught in the trap of inadequacy, he came face to face with shame and turned to God to lament. There was no validation, no affirmation, just petition to God for deliverance.

When all is said and done, who do you look to for deliverance from your cramps? How often do you take the cramps of life directly to God and ask Him to help you respond responsibly? Like David, you will find that God does hear you. He does see you. And He wants to deliver you. His truth and kindness are just a prayer away.

LISTEN TO: Deliver Me

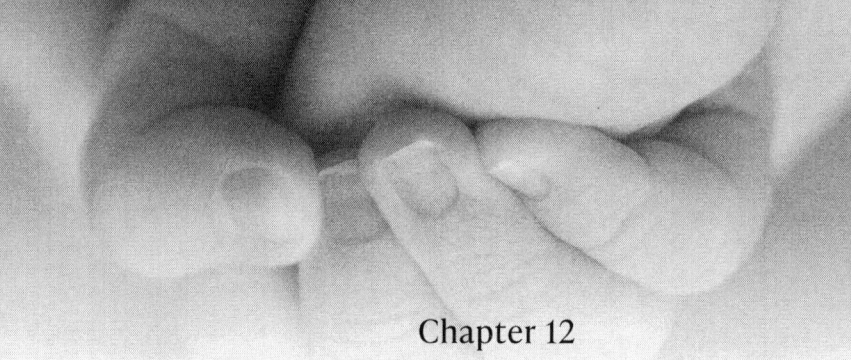

Chapter 12

I—DENTITY

> *I yam what I yam, and that's what I yam.*
> —**Popeye**

> *Christian selfhood is not defined in terms of who we are in and of ourselves. It's defined in terms of what God does to us and the relationship he creates with us and the destiny he appoints for us. God made us who we are so we could make known who he is. Our identity is for the sake of making known his identity.*
> —**John Piper from Christian Identity and Christian Destiny,** *Desiring God*

The 2018 top-selling Grammy Award-winning Christian song *You Say*, recorded by Lauren Daigle, expresses the doubts we have about not being enough. The song encourages us to replace those doubts with affirming messages of what God says about us instead. The song *I Am No Victim* recorded by Bethel Music's Kristen DeMarco, describes who we aren't. Take a further look at Christian magazines, books, blogs, podcasts, and you'll find identity in Christ to be a hot topic. Healing prayers and ministries coupled with sermons and studies on identity in Christ are filling churches in epic proportions. Psalm 139:14 *"I praise you, for I am fearfully and wonderfully made"*—has become a Christian anthem. In theory, we replace one negative message with a positive one. In practice, that positive message would be Scripture, a renewal of the mind.

Romans 10:2-4 urges, *"Do not be conformed to this world, but be transformed by the renewal of your mind, that by testing you may discern what is the will of God, what is good and acceptable and perfect.* 2 Corinthians 10:5 states: *We destroy arguments and every lofty opinion raised against the knowledge of God and take every thought captive to obey Christ."*

Indeed, replacing the enemy's message with God's Word is a great way to combat lies, and songs can be part of that process. However, before we go too far into this chapter, I want to offer a word of caution. Not every practice or affirming message is from God, even if it sounds "good." For example, New Thought philosophy believes in the Law of Attraction—the belief that positive or negative thoughts bring positive or negative experiences into a person's life. The idea is that if we just think positive things, positive things will happen. Be sure to seek wisdom from Scripture and the guidance of the Holy Spirit.

As we explore our identity and come up short, what ways do we seek out affirmations? Should they come from others, ourselves, or God?

Relationship with self

Jesus said in Luke 10:27, *"You shall love the Lord your God with all your heart and with all your soul and with all your strength and with all your mind, and your neighbor as **yourself**."* In this passage, Jesus is identifying three distinct relationships: 1) relationship with God,

Chapter 12 – I—Dentity

2) relationship with others, and 3) relationship with self. I've heard many Bible teachers interpret the "as yourself" in this verse to mean "do unto others." I'm not arguing that application, but I would like to add to it. Since what Jesus *didn't* say often causes us to pause, perhaps we can consider an additional application. Perhaps Jesus knew we would already love ourselves, but how do we love ourselves without appearing selfish?

Psychologists refer to the love relationship we have with ourselves as self-esteem. I would argue against using the word *esteem,* because I don't think Jesus is saying we need to esteem ourselves. Our tendency is to esteem ourselves too much. How should we think about ourselves?

Romans 12:3 tells us, *"For by the grace given to me I say to everyone among you not to think of himself more highly than he ought to think, but to think with sober judgment, each according to the measure of faith that God has assigned."*

In the Greek, *sober* is "sophron" and denotes the presence of soundness of thought. We can conclude that sober judgment means thoughtful, sound judgment of oneself. This implies awareness and ownership. Ownership requires repentance. As self-aware believers, we become more alert to our relationship with God, how we come across to others, and how we make things about us.

Self-awareness comes through acknowledgment. If we've told the story of our frame, fan club deficit, the shame of sin, or how we cramp our progress, we are aware, understand what we need to repent about, and no longer have a need to seek validation. By being aware of the dross in our life, we can better characterize when a conflict is about us or perhaps the other person. We no longer have as many needs as we once did. We forget what is behind and change our expectations. How do we get there?

Self-affirmation

Living with a firm grasp is a process that includes our concept of self. Let's be honest. It's challenging to love ourselves. We're limited, we make mistakes, and we sin. We've acted in ways or spoken words or experienced events that alter our view and send us straight into the Hall of Shame. Because we live with ourselves twenty-four-seven, we know more often when we miss the mark. When that happens, we love hearing others say nice things about us.

I don't know about you, but when someone gives me a compliment, expresses interest or takes notice, I find myself attracted to that person. There have been times words of affirmation have lingered in my soul like a lifeline. I've found myself re-reading an affirming text, voice message, or comment. At work, I have a "kudos file" among my email folders where I keep affirmations I've received from students or colleagues. When I have a tough day, I'll take a look in that folder to encourage myself.

Are there ways to appropriately affirm ourselves? Perhaps messages from sermons that remind us *I am a daughter of the King, I am a member of the Royal Family of God, I am not condemned* are helpful. Renewing our mind with Scripture verses is a great place to start. Unfortunately, we have to continually renew our minds since the affirmations we receive may be temporary. Is there another way?

Humanity and dichotomy

Since affirmations from others come and go, in our humanity, we inwardly fluctuate between feeling good and bad about ourselves. Ask any performer about the high he gets from the crowd, or the speaker who can't wait to speak again because he enjoys the applause. These kinds of experiences cause a rise and fall in our identity. Inevitably, when the feeling we don't measure up comes back again - and it

Chapter 12 – I—Dentity

will - we tend to seek affirming statements to counteract the bad. Our energy is then spent on feeding ourselves or feeding others so they will feed us.

When you get confused about who you are, I would encourage you to remember that until we meet Jesus, there are three things that make us human: Limitations, Mistakes, and Sins.

We all have limitations. It's part of being human. Not all of us can be on stage or be a star athlete. When we reflect on our limits, do we find ourselves being defensive or self-effacing? Or do we try to do something we're not gifted at because we like the attention it provides?

Mistakes are those things we do without ill intentions. Examples include spilling milk, forgetting to return library books, or adding up your bills incorrectly. When you make a mistake, do you try to hide it or beat yourself up about it? Do you offer an explanation, apologize, or make it right?

Sin is missing God's standards. This can be intentional, as in disobedience, or could be a faulty understanding of sin. When you sin and are called out on it, do you become defensive? Do you try to shame yourself or blame others?

In our quest to feel better about ourselves, we may shy away from discussing our limits, mistakes, and sins. It's not fun. However, the reality is that we are both good and bad. Paul describes this dichotomy in Romans 7:21-24. *"So, I discover this law: When I want to do what is good, evil is present with me. For in my inner self I delight in God's law, but I see a different law in the parts of my body, waging war against the law of my mind and taking me prisoner to the law of sin in the parts of my body. What a wretched man I am! Who will rescue me from this body of death?"*

Self-awareness is helpful in any of these scenarios. By categorizing our feelings of unworthiness as a limit, mistake, or sin, we can alter our response. Humility is the necessary first step. Accepting our dichotomy is another.

Where do we go?

Even though Paul expresses the dichotomy, our culture doesn't encourage us to live in discomfort. Society wants us to live in the feel-good-about-ourselves-whatever-it-takes side. Self-help, self-indulgence, and self-talk seems to satisfy our need. In the search for a healthy self-concept, we tend to choose activities that will help us escape or numb ourselves. We'll use technology as our drug of choice or binge on movies, video games, or abuse alcohol. Anything to escape the stresses of life, our ability to handle them, or what our limits, mistakes, or sins tell us about ourselves.

Social media demands more of us. According to *Our World in Data*, we spend at least six hours per day on social media. In an article written by Katie Moritz in "Rewire" magazine, the average adult spends close to eleven hours looking at a screen per day and will check their phone every ten minutes. Although contact with social media isn't necessarily sinful, it can keep us from the mission. As we tweet about where we're going, post videos about the details of our day, or argue about politics, we may be creating an insatiable need to see how many comments or likes we have. As we get attention, we experience pleasure, so we do it again - and again. Some of the research on Social Media Addiction validates this: "At Harvard University, researchers hooked people up to functional MRI machines to scan their brains and see what happens when they talk about themselves, which is a key part of what people do in social media. They found that self-disclosure communication stimulates the brain's pleasure centers, much like sex and food do."

As the cycle continues, we may self-isolate. But then we don't like feeling lonely, so we try to get attention. Although we want to relate,

Chapter 12 – I—Dentity

we get more and more anxious about meeting someone in person or even talking on the phone. During a pandemic, these patterns are amplified. Affirmations, numbing ourselves, and comparison lead us towards more isolation. At some point or other, we may come to terms with our limitations and mistakes, but we still have to wrestle with our identity as a sinner.

The wrestle

So how do we wrestle? Where do we wrestle? You may say, "Well, let's go to church. Church will meet the need. I will be accepted and affirmed there by anchoring myself in my identity in Christ." In my search for peace in this area, I honestly thought identity was the answer. Almost everything that happened to me—relational exchanges, work projects, or ministry goals—were now viewed through the lens of my "identity" *in* Christ. Isn't this what it means to have a firm grasp?

Personality tests became my next fix. I did the DISC, Meyer-Briggs, Strengths Finder, Enneagram, Colors Assessment, and Spiritual Gifts Assessments to learn more about myself. Each of them gave me a little more insight into my personality and explained some of my behavior patterns. Admittedly, I gained some enlightenment. I did feel a bit better about myself when I discovered others with the same profile and felt validated on some level. Still, deep down, the wrestle continued.

As years passed, I was drawn to a class at church which emphasized original design. The concept of original design was to anchor ourselves on a new vision—the vision God originally intended for us before sin entered the world. Doesn't that sound great? Who wants to dwell on our unworthiness? Indeed, to have victory in Christ meant we didn't let the brokenness of sin affect or define us. Victory achieved. Hallelujah!

The class included an original design prayer. The prayer's purpose was to help identify who God says we were originally before sin or the labels of brokenness entered our world. I was so excited, feeling this would surely satisfy! As I watched others being prayed over, each person left with a word from the Lord about who they are. Some of the affirming words I heard were cherished, admired, respected. These words from Abba Father seemed to bring healing to those who didn't receive validation from their earthly fathers. I watched as these words of affirmation flowed freely over others like a river quenching thirst. I couldn't wait to hear what God was going to say to me.

As those praying over me surrounded me, they asked what word kept coming to me. Friends, I could hardly believe my word—victim. Really?

As you may guess, this word sent me into a mental, emotional, and spiritual tailspin. From a human perspective, one could characterize me as a victim. After all, sexual exploitation, sexual abuse, racial violence, physical abuse, and financial insecurity qualify. Or maybe in the context of my father dying when I was ten, being sexually harassed, being bullied in the workplace, and living through the rejection of an ex-husband, I could see why some might call me a victim. But that didn't make me feel better about myself. It actually made me feel worse!

Although the intention beyond the prayer was freedom, all it did was make me angry. Confused, I asked God: Is that how You see me? Is that how others see me? Is that how I see myself? I latched onto the song "I Am No Victim" as my comfort. I continually renewed my mind through Scripture to counteract this negative description with something positive. It worked…for a while.

After six months of the give and take, I finally surrendered. That's when God revealed to me a colossal truth. Susan, you are a victim. Even though this self-awareness could have easily tempted me to linger in the Hall of Shame, instead it pivoted me somewhere else… somewhere more profound. God showed me the word *victim* wasn't His original design for me, but it was how sin had affected me. He invited me to *acknowledge* it, instead of fighting it. As mentioned in *The Frame* chapter, I needed to look back to understand what I needed to be saved from. Friends, God wasn't going to let this go; He was seeking to satisfy. This was my dross, this was my "it."

In therapist Sally Livingston's book, *Get Over It*, she describes the importance of defining our "it" through objectivity, observations, and remaining open to what God has for us. Why was I afraid to accept my identity as a victim? Didn't God want me to rest in His presence instead of my perceptions? The answer was a resounding *yes*! Friends, even though pursuing our identity isn't meaningless, let me save you some time. Don't spend so much of your "head space" wrapped up in figuring out who you are. Instead, embrace the fact you are a hybrid. You are a victim *and* a daughter of the King. You are a sinner *and* a saint. Noel Jesse Heikkinen's book, *Wretched Saints*, describes this wrestling. He says, "The truth of the Gospel of Jesus is this: I am nothing more than a wretch, and so much more than a saint."

At first glance, admitting we are sinners and have been sinned against appears counterintuitive. It's not very affirming. It doesn't make us feel good about ourselves. Not feeling good about ourselves ultimately means we are searching for approval over acknowledgment. Instead of replacing one message with another, what if we just acknowledged that both are true?

Unworthy

If God identifies us as humans who make mistakes, have limitations, and are sinners, why dwell on our unworthiness or how great we are? Many of the clients I see in lay counseling are going through life transitions. Transitions greatly affect our identity. Many want to feel better about their circumstances, but ultimately, they want to feel better about themselves. Many of them seek validation of their experience and want someone to tell them they are *not* unworthy… or that they deserve better. Although counseling sessions include encouragement, and especially acknowledgment, they also need to include deeper truths.

Let's get really honest. We *are* unworthy. We *have* missed the mark. We *are* sinners. And as humans, we *do have* limitations and make mistakes. What if we got comfortable with that? Matthew 9:13 teaches us, *"Go and learn what this means: 'I desire mercy, and not sacrifice.' For I came not to call the righteous, but sinners."*

I love the parable of the Prodigal, because Jesus offers us a glimpse into how God looks at us. This isn't a story of affirmation, but rather a story of how easily our occupation with our unworthiness can distract us. Luke 15:11-21 tells us:

> *And he said, "There was a man who had two sons. And the younger of them said to his father, 'Father, give me the share of property that is coming to me.' And he divided his property between them. Not many days later, the younger son gathered all he had and took a journey into a far country, and there he squandered his property in reckless living. And when he had spent everything, a severe famine arose in that country, and he began to be in need. So he went and hired himself out to one of the citizens of that country, who sent him into his fields to feed pigs. And he was longing to be fed with the pods that the pigs ate, and no one gave him anything. But when he came to himself, he said, 'How many of my father's hired servants have more than enough bread, but I perish here with hunger! I will arise and go to my father, and I will say to him, "Father, I have sinned*

against heaven and before you. I am no longer worthy to be called your son. Treat me as one of your hired servants."' And he arose and came to his father. But while he was still a long way off, his father saw him and felt compassion, and ran and embraced him and kissed him. And the son said to him, 'Father, I have sinned against heaven and before you. I am no longer worthy to be called your son.'"

Notice that the son said he was *no longer worthy*. Acknowledgment = validation. This is the son being self-aware enough to admit his sin. Doesn't salvation begin when we admit we're unworthy?

Friends, it's okay. Really, it is. Please take a few minutes to say it out loud so you get comfortable. *I am unworthy.* Say it again. But take notice. The story isn't over. Notice carefully how his father responds in verses 22-24:

But the father said to his servants, "Bring quickly the best robe, and put it on him, and put a ring on his hand, and shoes on his feet. And bring the fattened calf and kill it, and let us eat and celebrate. For this my son was dead, and is alive again; he was lost, and is found." And they began to celebrate.

Does the father dwell on his son's unworthiness? Does he even bring it up? Does he offer his son affirmation so he can feel better about his unworthiness? Friends, the story implies that the father had no interest in talking about his son's unworthiness –because the sin had already been acknowledged. His sin wasn't an issue for the father any longer because he heard his son acknowledge his unworthiness. Acknowledgment (validation) precedes celebration (affirmation)!

Mercy reigns

A beautiful picture of the mercy of our heavenly Father, this parable reminds us of the importance of validation. He knows we have limitations, make mistakes, and sin. But once we acknowledge our state, our unworthiness is not an issue between us and God any longer. Instead, He'd rather celebrate us. Why? Take a moment to be still and sit with this a minute: because God says *we're worth it!*

Each nail that was hammered into our Savior, each lash He received, each drop of His blood that fell to the earth sends this message. You may not be worthy, but you're worth it. Can you say *that* out loud? *"I am worth it!"* The challenge with figuring out our identity is that we aren't one thing. We are sinners and saints. We are wounded but healed. We are unworthy and worth it.

Why fight the dichotomy? Doesn't God understand dichotomy? While on earth, Jesus was in a dichotomous state—both God and man. How would our lives look different if we could rest in this dichotomy?

Friends, ultimately, the answer is mercy. Mercy is bigger than a promotion, a book deal, being a star, or having a fan club. Mercy is bigger than our inadequacies, our frame, or the way we respond. We may make vows, cramp our mission, and fall into Satan's traps, but mercy is offered to us freely. Mercy is offered to us daily.

Default system

In order to get a firm grasp and rest in God's dichotomous view of you, you may have to make some adjustments. You may have to change your settings. In a previous chapter, we discussed our MDS, our Message Default System. This is the message system to which we typically default, especially in times of stress. This system includes that box of negative messages we've been trying to fight against and

Chapter 12 – I—Dentity

may include our coping strategies. When we default to our past, we remember we aren't stars, have no fan club, are trapped in inadequacy, make vows we break, and linger in the Hall of Shame. As long as we see ourselves as *only* unworthy, we will be easily offended or passionately defensive, leading to an excessive need for validation or affirmation.

Click the reset button. Change your default to the Mercy Response System (MRS). Real, authentic, life-transforming affirmation happens at the cross. Micah 6:8 tells us, *"He has told you, O man, what is good; and what does the Lord require of you but to do justice, and to love kindness, and to walk humbly with your God?"*

A story from *Our Daily Bread* entitled *Running from Sin*, on Bible.org, sheds some light on the subject.

The story is told of a young girl who accepted Christ as her Savior and applied for membership in a local church. "Were you a sinner before you received the Lord Jesus into your life?" inquired an old deacon. "Yes, sir," she replied. "Well, are you still a sinner?"

"To tell you the truth, I feel I'm a greater sinner than ever." "Then what real change have you experienced?" "I don't quite know how to explain it," she said, "except I used to be a sinner running after sin, but now that I am saved, I'm a sinner running from sin!"

Instead of figuring out *who* you are, may you rest in *whose* you are. Your identity isn't in Christ—your identity **IS** Christ.

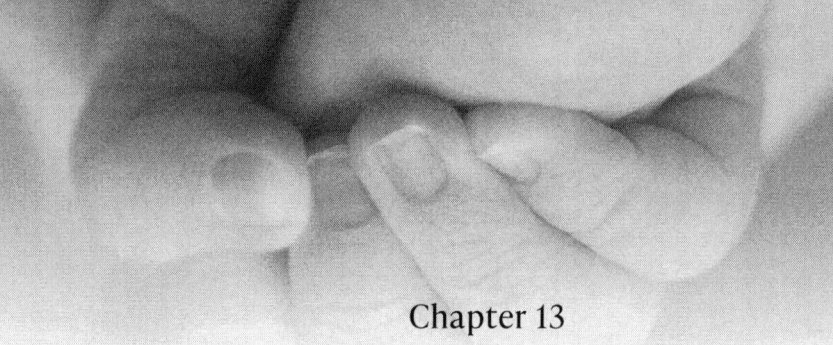

Chapter 13

THE SEESAW

———————— " ————————

Patty: I'll be the good guy.
Shermy: I'll be the bad guy.
Patty: What are you going to be, Charlie Brown?
Charlie Brown: I'll be sort of in-between; I'll be a hypocrite!
—**Charles M. Schulz, The Complete Peanuts, Vol. 1: 1950-1952**

He desperately wants you to know Him. So many people believe in God, but they don't really know Him. And because they don't really know Him, they are lukewarm. The truth is, if you truly knew Him, you couldn't be lukewarm or halfhearted. If you remain lukewarm, maybe it's because you don't know who God really is.
—**Craig Groeschel**, *Weird: Because Normal Isn't Working*

When you jump across a canyon, cautious, small steps and vacillation won't work. Sometimes you just have to go for it.
—**Rick Warren**

Do you remember the last time you saw a seesaw? You know, the old-fashioned kind. Along with the slide, swing, and merry-go-round, the seesaw won a coveted place in playgrounds worldwide. A seesaw is a plank where two children sit on opposite ends; when one goes up, the other goes down. The point of the seesaw is to find the right balance. Two children can enjoy going up and down or try to balance. If one child weighs more than the other, the heavier one will have to move closer to the center to achieve balance. If two children are roughly the same weight, the seesaw will balance because they're exerting equal and oppositely directed forces. As a child, I never knew I could adjust myself closer to the center, so I avoided seesaws. (I'm sure my counselor may be able to shed some light on that one.)

Seesaws remind us of the ups and downs of life and how we struggle to find balance. When we are experiencing one emotion, we typically seesaw to the opposite emotion to counterbalance. Even in society, we do the same thing. An example is diets. First, we're told eggs are terrible for us and then we are told they are good for us. Vacillating between extremes, it seems to be human nature to go the polar opposite. By viewing a situation from two very opposite viewpoints, we often get stuck deciding where to land.

When I was a teenager, a friend called me wishy-washy. At first, I wasn't exactly sure what she meant, but I think it was because I couldn't make up my mind. When I finally did, I would quickly regret my choice. I'm confident it drove her crazy, but for me, there was always another way to look at the situation. I didn't want to disappoint anyone with my choices. I lived in fear of their response. I didn't have a firm grasp.

As we think about our lives, and our dichotomy, achieving balance is tricky. When we feel ignored, we search for attention. When we're not confident, we can become indecisive or cocky. When we feel shame, it may look like pride. Consider these seesaw examples.

Chapter 13 – The Seesaw

Validation and empathy

We have defined validation as an acknowledgment of our experience. Remember, validation doesn't mean we agree or approve, but rather, we respect the person's right to their experience even if it's different from ours. We don't necessarily have to live the same experiences as the other person to validate them.

The other side of the seesaw is empathy. Translated from the German word *einfühlung, empathy* is a combination of two Greek words, *em* and *pathos*. Together they mean *in feeling*. Empathy is the ability to feel what someone else is feeling.

Recently, I needed major surgery due to a biopsy that indicated cancerous cells. This was a time I needed empathy and validation. The surgery would further identify how much cancer was present and how far it had spread. I was concerned, but kept trusting God would equip me whatever the results. Cards, flowers, good wishes, and prayers were showered on me before, during, and after surgery. As others extended empathy and validation to me, I found it awkward receiving this kind of attention. As I became more comfortable being vulnerable, I was fascinated by the difference in how others offered empathy. I saw three distinct styles—cognitive, emotional, and compassionate.

When someone offers cognitive empathy, they offer it through thought rather than feeling. My daughter expresses this by asking specific questions about the surgery, the process, and next steps. Others were more aware of my emotional feelings and fears. The final group had to do something—anything—like bring over food or help with chores to show their compassion. Each of those displays of empathy blessed me, but in a different way.

Believe it or not, I didn't feel a strong need for others to offer empathy. I needed validation. I needed others to acknowledge my cancer experience. Validating someone's experience is crucial to building trust and showing love. Indeed, the ability to see someone's situation from their perspective is helpful, but does this mean we have to feel the same emotion they feel?

The social psychologist C. Daniel Batson, who has researched empathy for decades, argues that empathy can now refer to eight different concepts: "knowing another's thoughts and feelings; imagining another's thoughts and feelings; adopting the posture of another; actually feeling as another does; imagining how one would feel or think in another's place; feeling distress at another's suffering; feeling for another's suffering, sometimes called pity or compassion; and projecting oneself into another's situation."

With all those definitions, would you say our need for deep level empathy is realistic to receive? For example, let's say you are in a car accident and break your leg. Even if someone else had a similar experience and broke their leg, they may not have broken it the same way. Circumstances surrounding the accident were different. How you broke the leg may be different. How you respond to the broken leg may be different. Often, we think someone is not empathetic because they can't feel exactly what we feel. We conclude others can't truly understand what we're going through because their experience is different. Could we be expecting empathy when they are offering validation? Can we embrace acknowledgment as being enough?

As believers, we're called to share in the suffering of our brothers and sisters. In Romans 12:15, Paul tells us, *"Rejoice with those who rejoice, and weep with those who weep."* We're also called to compassion. 1 Peter 3:8 says, *"Finally, all of you, be like-minded and show sympathy, love, compassion, and humility to and for each other."* And we're called to comfort each other in 2 Corinthians 1:3-4, which says, *"Blessed be the God and Father of our Lord Jesus Christ, the Father of mercies and God of all comfort, who comforts us in all our affliction, so that we may be able to comfort those who are in any affliction, with the comfort with which we ourselves are comforted by God."* Do we have to offer one and not the other? Couldn't we offer both?

Affirmation and approbation

We have defined affirmation as an approval or celebration of our experience. The challenging part is what happens when we don't get approval. If someone disapproves, does this mean they are not empathetic?

Approbation is the lust for attention. Some have more of a tendency towards this lust pattern than others. As mentioned in other chapters, a predisposition towards narcissism can look like a lust pattern but it could be a mental illness. For others, it may be wanting to be the alpha in the room or a desire to have the last word. We may seek out activities that will put us on a public platform rather than behind the scenes. We may easily become jealous when others receive attention, and we don't. Some of us just like to hear ourselves talk.

As the "dross" in your life rises to the surface, and you become more self-aware, you'll understand how to balance between these extremes. Desiring affirmation is human. Lusting after it is extreme.

Shame and pride

Pride has stumped philosophers and theologians for centuries. We applaud self-reliance, determination, and individualism and encourage these traits with gold stars and blue ribbons. Certainly, it's okay to be proud of our accomplishments, but at what point do we take it to the other extreme? When is it too much pride?

In the June Issue of "Current Directions in Psychological Science," psychologists experimented with the idea of two faces of pride. Authentic pride and hubristic pride.

Authentic pride manifests itself through individuals who feel those positive, achievement-oriented feelings about their hard work. Individuals exhibiting this kind of pride scored high in areas of adaptability, extraversion, self-awareness, and conscientiousness. They felt as though they had the power of choice.

On the other hand, hubristic (excessive) pride has its roots in shame. Individuals exhibiting this kind of pride feel that success is predetermined. You're either talented or not. They also tended to overinflate their talents and relentlessly sought out approbation. Because of their shame, they created fantasies about their accomplishments.

In the chapter *Enter the Hall*, unmasking shame is a crucial step in getting a firm grasp. If you see defensiveness, depression, anger, pride or bitterness behind your decisions, you can be sure shame is at the root. If you're vacillating between pride and shame, now you know why.

In *Avatar: The Last Airbender,* Uncle Iroh said, "Pride is not the opposite of shame, but its source. True humility is the only antidote to shame."

Inferiority and superiority

Swinging between feelings of inferiority and superiority became the seesaw ride of my life. When I would win an audition, I felt better than others. When I lost, I felt like the world had fallen apart. When I made a mistake, I concluded I wasn't good enough for any job. Comparison became my seesaw.

It's common to have nagging feelings of self-doubt when we don't attain a goal. We're not talking about those isolated moments, but those continued exaggerated feelings of not measuring up. Sometimes, we may create a false concept in our mind that someone thinks a certain way about us. Scripture reminds us in Romans 12:3, *"For by the grace given to me I say to everyone among you not to think of himself more highly than he ought to think, but to think with sober judgment, each according to the measure of faith that God has assigned."* Sober judgment equals self-awareness.

Hypervigilance and passiveness

In Chapter 2, we discussed hypervigilance in more detail. Hypervigilance takes vigil on everything, almost looking like perfectionism. Behind it may be a desire to have the edge on everyone else or be one step ahead to self-protect. Hypervigilance exaggerated can appear prideful. Boldness moves forward while passiveness holds back. Boldness takes action while passiveness refuses to engage. Hypervigilance is extreme boldness.

The other side of the seesaw is a passive person. Passiveness is more than laziness. A passive person will hold back and let others act. Behind it can be a desire to avoid the feeling of not accomplishing a goal or feeling like they won't measure up. John Piper describes a passive person as one who exhibits self-pity."The reason self-pity does not look like pride is that it appears to be so needy. But the need arises from a wounded ego. It doesn't come from a sense of unworthiness, but from a sense of unrecognized worthiness. It is the response of un-applauded pride"

Balance

So how do we achieve a balance? By getting a firm grasp. When we understand we are not worthy and worth it at the same time, we accept our hybrid life. We realize we don't have to go to extremes because two things can happen at the same time. Rick Warren said in an article by Relevant Magazine, "Life is like a set of railroad tracks. Rather than life being hills and valleys, I believe that it's kind of like two rails on a railroad track, and at all times you have something good and something bad in your life."

It seems we keep reaching for this holy grail, this holy balance. I've never met anyone who has a completely balanced life. Do genuine happiness and contentment come from achieving perfect balance? Or do they come from knowing how to make your expectations fit your circumstances? Getting comfortable with both sides of the seesaw may end up providing the balance we're seeking. Maybe it will help us stop being defensive or getting offended easily. Go ahead and enjoy the ride.

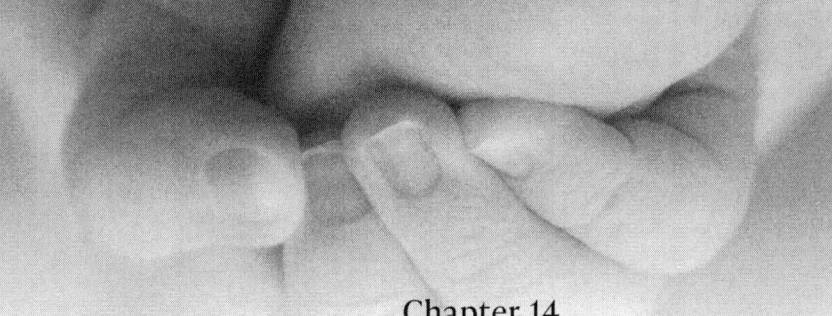

Chapter 14

OFFENSE OR DEFENSE

"

The feeling of being "offended" is a warning indicator that is showing you where to look within yourself for unresolved issues.
—Bryant H. McGill

There are times when explanations, no matter how reasonable, just don't seem to help.
—Fred Rogers

If you are on a continuous search to be offended, you will always find what you are looking for; even when it isn't there.
—Bill Kellogg

As announcements blared, the pep band was warming up, referees were positioning themselves, coaches were strategizing, and athletes were bouncing balls on the court. I could smell the sweat in the arena. Yes, it was basketball season.

A Firm GRASP

Although I didn't play basketball competitively, I've always enjoyed the game; and I especially like watching sports when I know someone on the team. Although my daughters were musical, and I went to many concerts, they didn't play competitive sports. When I married my husband, his three children were involved in sports, and one was even a Division 1 basketball player. I was excited to have the opportunity to be a fan!

Getting a basketball scholarship to college is no small feat. Years of training, practicing, and additional tournaments outside of school are necessary to develop that level of athleticism. Of course, we all love watching our team win, especially when they get a winning basket at the buzzer, (which, by the way, happened to my stepson twice.) I rejoiced when they won and empathized when they lost. However, as I got to know the game of basketball better, I learned more about game strategy—what makes a good pass, how to see the court, and the importance of good defense. Some will argue that offense is more important because the one who has more points wins the game. Yet, defense is just as vital as it minimizes the opponent's possession time and shooting percentage. Both are important to winning a game, especially at the collegiate level.

But frankly, I'm just a spectator. And, boy, do we spectators have opinions. How easy it is to criticize the coaches, offer a better game plan, or shout out stats. Over the years, I've come to see what we say about our teams and their players reflects a lot about the way we think.

Yet in life, we don't always think about a game plan. We just respond. And feel justified. We tend to go on the offense or defense towards our circumstances, others, and even God.

Measurements

One of the best ways to measure our mindset in this area is how easily we are offended. Offenses can reveal wounds, sin nature tendencies, and judgments. Acting on judgments can hinder our relationships with God, others, and ourselves. How do we measure up? What are our stats?

Measuring my offensive and defensive tendencies was one of the best ways I became aware of my validation and affirmation deficit. As I observed my response to an event or person, I began to realize how easily I was offended. I became aware of how defensive I became. Could this response be based on my Message Default System (MDS)?

Responding strictly with our MDS can be faulty, or maybe inconsistent at best. By replacing one message with another, we build spiritual skills. However, if we don't reset, we end up going back to our default. This is where self-awareness is key.

As you look at the following questions, keep in mind these questions are *not* about measuring your actions, but rather your attitude or mindset. Is your response originating from messages or mercy?

1) How do you respond when someone doesn't agree with you?

In the Facets chapter, we explored how everyone has a different way of observing the world. Do you get offended when someone views the world through another facet? Do you sulk, enter the Hall of Shame, get angry, or feel resentful? Do you act "holier than thou"? Or do you vehemently try to defend your position by attacking theirs?

When resting in the Mercy Response System (MRS), you live at peace, knowing that someone else can view the world differently. You embrace their *right* to choose their viewpoint, even though you may not agree with them. Mercy loves to understand.

2) How do you respond when someone gives you feedback?

Has anyone ever told you that you take things personally? Or that you are defensive? Though we all have blind spots, we may not like what someone else says about us. We get offended and pronounce them wrong. Or we get defensive, usually attacking the other person or offering detailed explanations.

Mercy understands that our unworthiness is a fact, not a life sentence. Mercy isn't surprised by limitations, mistakes, or sin. Mercy embraces feedback as a way to identify how we can serve each other better.

3) How do you respond when someone challenges things in your life that are important to you?

On "The Notice" podcast, one of my guests was Pastor Jack Magruder. He discussed how this question can help us identify idols in our life. "When someone thinks you're wrong, do you become angry, self-righteous, or judgmental? Do you defend your right to have whatever it is? "

Mercy embraces change. Mercy desires priorities to be in sync with the mission.

Real or imagined

Another way to measure our strategies is to distinguish between a real or imagined offense. Let's consider white privilege as an example. When someone labeled me as having white privilege, I was initially offended. As I processed it, I measured it. I discovered there is something about it that is "real" because white privilege is real. What was "imagined" was the character assassination of myself that the term implied. As I took it personally, I immediately defended my experiences. After all, I grew up in Detroit's racially tense streets, had friends of color, and certainly didn't have the kind of money that would imply I was privileged. How could someone put that label on me?

Actually, the conversation wasn't really about me, but I successfully made it about me. It was more about the other person and their concerns and attitudes regarding white privilege. After further discussion, it became apparent that our definition of the term was different. Gaps in understanding may cause us to imagine an offense when that wasn't the intention.

Generally speaking, when we are offended, we make a judgment that the other person isn't validating us. When someone expresses *their* perspective—how they view the issue from their facet—why are we quick to try to change their perspective? Or why do we insist on having to share ours? 2 Corinthians 10:5 explains, *"We destroy arguments and every lofty opinion raised against the knowledge of God and take every thought captive to obey Christ."*

Friends, by accepting ourselves as dichotomous beings, we focus best when we understand God validates us. When we choose to destroy arguments, or lofty opinions, we recognize how God acknowledges our experiences in a way no one else can. After all, He knows our entire story. As we become self-aware enough of those arguments, it frees us to focus on the job of loving others and validating them instead of seeking validation for ourselves.

Methods

Whether the offense is real or imagined, we tend to respond using one of two methods—offense (passivity) and defense (attack).

Victim mode is offensive because it assumes no one understands us or our experience. We feel like a misfit or claim "woe is me." We act like we want validation (acknowledgement), when in reality, we want vindication (clearing of blame).

Ironically, this is a passive strategy because we are letting the other person solve the problem while we shut down. We do this by holding a grudge, becoming overly anxious, procrastinating, or acting insecure. We may even be overly nice while interpreting every negative interaction as a victimization incident. We might even call this emotional upset "trauma."

Keep in mind, when I speak of being a victim, I am not talking about victims, like in the Larry Nassar sexual abuse case, who are requiring a perpetrator to take responsibility for their actions. This kind of response reflects a fantastic amount of courage as victims seek equality, accountability, and justice. I'm speaking about the type of offense where we rest in our victimhood, waiting for someone to give us vindication or validation. Or we seek affirmation because they aren't vindicating us.

The other method is aggression. Typically, we attack to defend or protect ourselves. This method comes across in the following ways: a "holier-than-thou" attitude, teaching or preaching, sarcasm, criticism, endless explaining or rationalizing, trivializing the effect, jumping to conclusions, or blaming the other person. When someone tells us something about ourselves that we don't like to hear, we even tell them their viewpoints are wrong.

The problem with both of these methods is that we aren't taking responsibility for our response to the real or imagined offense. Instead, we blame others through passive or aggressive behaviors. We then feel justified to gossip or slander because we need to protect ourselves.

Friends, of course we have no control over the behavior or statements others make, nor can we stop racists from hating, or sexists from denigrating, or elitists from power trips. But we can manage one person—*ourselves*.

Self-management

As mentioned previously, "respond-ability" is the ability to respond responsibly. You can take responsibility for your response by managing yourself. Self-control is a fruit of the spirit. We are reminded of the divine establishment principle of free will when we activate choice.

For example, let's say you're at a social gathering where you feel a little uncomfortable. You hear laughter from a separate conversation. Do you assume the people are laughing about you? Or maybe you've emailed someone, and they haven't responded. Do you assume the worst about them? As Eleanor Roosevelt said, "No one can make you feel inferior without your permission."

Here's the thing. We get a choice. We don't have to assume the worst, feel inferior or live as if we are victims, waiting for the other shoe to drop. We don't have to be on the attack in order to protect ourselves. We don't have to take things personally. Without self-management, we fail because we think the situation is all about us. Most times it's not. No, we can't change how a person will respond to us. They have "respond-ability" too. But we can rest in the power of choice—ours.

MRS

So how can we stop being offended? How can we receive feedback constructively? By using the Mercy Response System (MRS). The MRS replaces our MDS.

The first step is to receive. Receive the mercy of God for yourself. We do this by acknowledging our unworthiness. We can then offer mercy when attempting to understand if another person is coming from a broken place. We can offer mercy by letting go of our feelings and listening to the hurt behind others. When we respond with mercy, we tend to look at what others are saying about us as a behavior we can change, not a direct attack on our personhood. Mercy considers other facets. That person may be looking at the situation from the perspective of an unbeliever, who doesn't see from an eternal point of view—and we can't expect that of an unbeliever.

Friends, if the feedback you receive—from any source, whether believer or unbeliever—is something God wants you to address, He will make it clear. He will gently send the message multiple ways, so you know it's from Him. If it's not, we can't convince or demand someone to change their perspective. It's truth to them. 1 Corinthians 2:14 tells us, *"The natural person does not accept the things of the Spirit of God, for they are folly to him, and he is not able to understand them because they are spiritually discerned."*

I also encourage you not to be surprised by sin in an unbeliever's life. The best response to offer a non-believer is still mercy—the essence of the gospel.

If an offense you receive is from a believer, be sure to check it with God's Word to determine if it's a sin. Mistakes and limitations are human and should be given a mercy pass. If it is a sin, then Jesus gave us incredible teaching in Matthew 18:15-17 about what to do within the family of God to address those conflicts.

> *If your brother sins against you, go and tell him his fault, between you and him alone. If he listens to you, you have gained your brother. But if he does not listen, take one or two others along with you, that every charge may be established by the evidence of two or three witnesses. If he refuses to listen to them, tell it to the church. And if he refuses to listen even to the church, let him be to you as a Gentile and a tax collector.*

Notice the intention is to gain back your brother. It's not to make us feel better or prove someone else wrong. If we do this with the right intent, our eyes are not on ourselves, except to be aware of our own responsibility in the matter. By addressing that person in humility, we show mercy. Notice that Jesus did not say to get even, punish, or damage someone's reputation. That would be a violation of one of the Ten Commandments about bearing false witness. Ultimately, if the offender doesn't see his sin, let him go.

Here are some other ways to extend mercy:

- † Offer mercy when the other person's reaction may reflect pressure in his or her life.

- † Offer mercy when the other person's response may reflect their exhaustion.

- † Offer mercy when the other person's response may be due to their own concentration on issues, problems, or plans.

- † Offer mercy because the other person may be hurting.

- † Offer mercy to yourself because you may not see things clearly or you may misinterpret something.

- † Offer mercy to yourself if you see that you are being too sensitive or that your expectations are unreasonable.

- † Offer mercy to yourself when you discover the other person may just not like you.

- † Offer mercy to yourself when you may have done or said something to cause the person to react the way he or she did.

Finally, and most important of all, turn to God for affirmation, remembering He sees the offense. Psalm 34:18 tells us, *"The LORD is close to the brokenhearted and saves those who are crushed in spirit."*

If you still find yourself on the offense or defense after all this, you may not be seeking an end to the conflict, but instead wanting others' approval. Jade Mazarin, in his article for *Relevant Magazine*, said, "You see, that nagging desire to get responses from others is not actually about those other people. What it's really about is how you feel about yourself. If you are on a quest for another person's approval—it's because there's a part of you that doesn't completely approve of yourself."

Our example

In Scripture, Jesus was tempted in every way all of us are tempted, which includes the desire for approval. Yet, He chose to stay on mission with unshakeable confidence. Although He had many opportunities to be offended, Jesus responded differently than us. Why? Because He thought differently about it.

1) Jesus didn't need to be liked.

He was insulted, criticized, and told what to do many times. One person who seemed to want to challenge Jesus was Martha. Irritated, frustrated, and resentful, Martha felt justified in her self-righteousness. So much so that she even told Jesus what to do in Luke 10:40: *"But Martha was distracted with much serving. And she went up to him and said, 'Lord, do you not care that my sister has left me to serve alone? Tell her then to help me'."*

Martha didn't seem to like Jesus so much at that time. But Jesus wasn't concerned with her feelings about Him; He was more concerned about Martha's perspective. He saw her. Notice how Jesus validated Martha in Luke 10:41-42: *"But the Lord answered her, 'Martha, Martha, you are anxious and troubled about many things, but one thing is necessary. Mary has chosen the good portion, which will not be taken away from her'."*

When we listen to the voice that tells us we're unworthy, those feelings of not being liked can easily surface. But when we are more like Jesus, genuinely secure within, knowing we are a hybrid, we don't need validation to make us feel worthy.

2) Jesus knew who He was.

Jesus didn't exhaust Himself looking for a fan club, becoming a star, or getting caught in the trap of inadequacy. He didn't spend His time searching for His identity. He already knew He was a star, had a fan club, and was a dichotomous being—man and God at the same time. He already understood the balance between humility and self-worth. He already experienced the validation and affirmation that came through the community of the Trinity—Father, Son, and Spirit. Philippians 2:6 tells us, *"Who, though he was in the form of God, did not count equality with God a thing to be grasped."*

3) Jesus was able to separate the feelings of others from His own.

Jesus deeply understood and applied Luke 6:45 which tells us, *"Out of the heart the mouth speaks."*

Going back to Martha, Jesus separated her feelings from His. He could have responded by getting offended or defensive because she was so demanding. He applied boundaries by being self-aware enough to know where His feelings begin and hers ended. He responded by showing her a better way to view the situation and encouraging her to stay on mission. But He started the whole exchange out by validating where she was at.

Would we be so quick to feel offended if we remembered that other's behaviors and words are a reflection of them, not us? Would we receive re-direction if at first we were acknowledged?

4) Jesus stayed on mission because He loved the Father.

Jesus had one goal: To please the Father. He focused on what God needed Him to do. When we focus on seeking God's desires and carrying them out, we don't have the time to focus on other people's opinions. Their opinions become a non-issue in our lives.

A person's behavior reflects their inner world and their MDS, including their frame, shame, vows, inadequacies, and the ways they may have cramped their purpose. When someone acts rudely, it typically comes from a multitude of sources that have nothing to do with you.

Admonishment

Admonishment is a reprimand. If this happens to you, take notice. Proverbs 10:17 tells us, *"Whoever heeds instruction is on the path to life, but he who rejects reproof leads others astray."*

Admonishment provides accountability and encourages self-awareness. Admonishment is a gift. We need others in our lives who can point out our blind spots. However, if we have too much of a validation and affirmation deficit, we may not be open to correction. We may interpret the love and intent of a fellow believer who admonishes us as an attack. We may accuse them of not being safe when they are simply pointing out something to consider.

However, when done correctly, admonishment leads the other to obedience. Ideally, it would look like Colossians 3:16:*"Let the word of Christ dwell in you richly, teaching and admonishing one another in all wisdom, singing psalms and hymns and spiritual songs, with thankfulness in your hearts to God."*

Even when admonishment is not presented lovingly, God can still use it—if we're open to correction. When someone points out a blind spot or a sin, we can respond with humility centered on mercy. Respond-ability is the game plan.

Ironically, many of the best teams consist of players who are open to correction. The temptation for church members is to harden their hearts against those called to speak the truth in love. They may grow embittered against those who point out their sins and challenge them to walk worthy of the gospel they hold.

Chapter 14 – Offense or Defense

Our culture's message is this: Whatever you do, I will accept it, I will approve of it, for love requires agreement. Such a naïve statement endorses someone's road to hell. Rather, Paul teaches us to live and labor for the eternal good of others. Love requires truth. This love includes biblically grounded, Spirit-empowered admonition. Don't let yourself become offended. Don't let yourself be defensive.

Timothy Keller said, "Love without truth is sentimentality; it supports and affirms us but keeps us in denial about our flaws. Truth without love is harshness; it gives us information but in such a way that we cannot really hear it. God's saving love in Christ, however, is marked by both radical truthfulness about who we are and yet also radical, unconditional commitment to us. The merciful commitment strengthens us to see the truth about ourselves and repent. The conviction and repentance move us to cling to and rest in God's mercy and grace."

Let me leave you with a simple strategy: If I've ever offended you, I apologize. If you've ever offended me, I don't remember. In the end, Lord, teach me how to love.

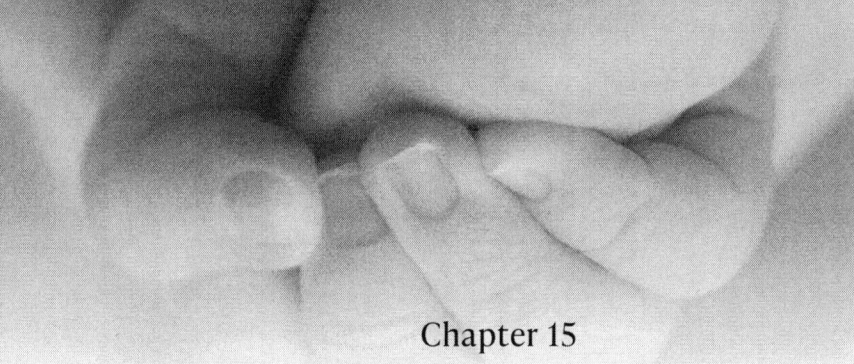

Chapter 15

THE WHY

❝

*Many of our deepest motives come not from an
adult logic of how things work in the world, but out
of something that is frozen from childhood.*
—**Kazuo Ishiguro**

*Many deceptions only appeal to us because there is
something inside us that "wants" to believe them.
They are seductive because of darkness and wrong
motives in our own lives. We must search our hearts
and root these out.*
—**Andrew Strom**

"We would like to hear number three and number seven," the audition proctor announced backstage. "To all others, thank you for coming." Over fifty clarinetists were auditioning for one clarinet position with a regional orchestra that paid approximately $3,000 annually. Many came from all over the country. Two got to the finals, and only one won the spot.

As a classical musician, competition is stiff for all jobs, even ones making little money. Reaching full-time status primarily as a performer is rare, just as rare as becoming a professional athlete. Most musicians have "portfolio careers," a combination of various sources of income streams. In my case, I perform, teach, and work in arts administration. Throughout my career, I've served in one, two, or all three of these capacities.

During one season of my career, I took a very demanding administrative position to meet my financial needs after divorce. I worked sixty plus hours per week, leaving little time to perform. After six-plus years, my financial picture changed. My daughters graduated from college, and I remarried, so I took a new job, allowing more time to perform. How exciting to return to my first love!

However, as things go in this profession, there are few opportunities and enormous competition. I got on a few sub-lists for paid orchestras and began an adjunct teaching position, so I was on my way back. However, even though pay wasn't involved, I decided to join the local concert band. Why? At the time, I felt it would be a good place to get back into playing shape, meet new people and "give back." Or so I thought.

At first glance, I was at peace with my decision. However, the core level and experience of the other musicians weren't at the level I typically performed. Even though I enjoyed getting to know the kind, interesting people who participate in community bands, I struggled. On some level, I guess it was affirming they were happy to have me and asked me to solo with the band. Yet after every rehearsal on the car ride home, the same thoughts ran through my head: "I can't believe how out of tune this band is. Did I really practice all these years to end up here? I know I'm not perfect, but what kind of person does that make me if I think I'm thinking I'm too good to be here?"

To resolve this internal struggle, I decided to anchor myself in my third reason for participating—the concept of giving back. Somehow

Chapter 15 – The Why

being noble felt affirming. When my nobility turned into frustration, I found myself complaining and impatient when the music didn't flow. To combat my frustration, I kept reminding myself of the individuals who gave of their time and talents to help me succeed. Surely, I could pay it forward.

As John Piper put it, "God is most glorified in us when we are most satisfied in Him." Because I was trying to be self-aware, I had to ask myself whether God was being glorified. Was I satisfied?

The answer was a resounding no. I didn't exhibit the fruits of the Spirit much either. It seemed I had two choices. Change my attitude or quit the band. I wasn't sure what God was trying to do in me, so I did what I usually do when there's a struggle—adjust myself.

Some rehearsals were better than others. I learned to hold my tongue and not verbalize my thoughts or make negative facial expressions. This became challenging when others around me complained. I don't think anyone in the band picked up on my frustration or would characterize me as a complainer, but I knew. And God knew. Externally, I changed my actions, but internally, I still had a bad attitude.

For some reason, this situation reminded me of a counseling appointment I had in college. I remembered the counselor explaining to me about hedonism. When you are a hedonist, you are motivated by pleasure. When you are altruistic, you are motivated by others, even to the point of self-denial. Since I wasn't participating in the band for my own pleasure, could I have been doing it for altruistic reasons? On some level, did I think paying it forward was altruistic? I didn't want either one of these motivators to dictate my decisions, so I conceded that maybe I was just thinking about it way too much. What difference does my why make?

Motives

One of the trickiest and most overlooked aspects of Christian living is our motives. We don't always think about our why, or we don't know why we do what we do. The Apostle Paul could identify with us. In Romans 7:15, he wrote, *"I do not understand my own actions. For I do not do what I want, but I do the very thing I hate."*

Although he was not looking specifically at motives, he was trying to understand himself. He was trying to be self-aware. Why would he do sinful things even though he wanted to do holy things? Proverbs 16:2 (NIV) tells us, *"All a person's ways seem pure to them, but motives are weighed by the Lord."*

Our motives can be complicated, but they do matter. Changing what we do overtly can be a step of obedience, but God knows our heart's motives, even more than we do. Friends, you can't run from God. He is the only one who truly notices *all* of you. He is not only with us twenty-four-seven, but He has access to the innermost thoughts and intents of our hearts. Can we get more noticed than that?

Others are only capable of observing our overt actions, oftentimes judging our motives. How can they know for sure if they can't see the intent of our hearts?

We can't talk about motives without talking about transactional relationships. Transactional relationships are typically motivated by function and money. Based on an exchange of money, goods, or services, they usually serve an exact point. When that point no longer makes sense, the relationship ends. A simple example of a transactional relationship is buying a car. Once you buy the car, your relationship with the salesman ends. You need a car, and the salesman needs money. There is no need to bond or become best friends. It's a simple, transactional exchange.

Chapter 15 – The Why

However, sometimes we look at our more intimate relationships as transactional. We may want something from another person, doing something for them so they'll do something for us. You know, I'll scratch your back if you scratch mine. A man might think if he's kind to his wife, she'll be more interested in sex. A person might think if they spend more time with a parent, the parent will think they're a good child. If we treat our close relationships as transactions, the relationship will eventually turn sour.

If motives are reasons behind our actions, is it possible to be motivated for both good and bad reasons? Couldn't we choose to do something good for the wrong reasons or something bad for good reasons?

Weaknesses and strengths

Romans 8:8 says,*"Those who are in the realm of the flesh cannot please God."*

In order to become more self-aware of our motives, it's helpful to understand that our sinful nature includes both a good and bad side. There are four distinct sin categories: overt, mental attitude, sins of the tongue, and self-indulgence.

Overt sins are obvious and include things like murder, adultery, drunkenness, or stealing. Mental attitude sins manifest as pride, jealousy, bitterness, hatred, vindictiveness, envy, guilt, fear, worry, anxiety, and self-pity. Sins of the tongue include accusing, judging, bullying, gossiping, and criticizing. Self-indulgence is living a life motivated strictly by pleasure.

Our sinful nature's human-good side has a few different looks. First, it likes to justify sin as being done for a good, altruistic reason. It can also show up as self-righteousness, pride, and even self-denial for the "good of the cause." Yes, God says to feed the hungry, house the homeless, give to the poor, and act kindly; but we may have to deny ourselves to accomplish these things. Sometimes that denial is motivated by altruism. Maybe we like to appear more giving than others or love the affirmation we get when others talk about the great things we did! Although denying ourselves isn't wrong, it can lead to resentment or bitterness if done for the wrong reasons.

In the old nursery rhyme "The Queen of Hearts," the Knave of Hearts steals the queen's tarts to give to the poor. This is an example of a wrong thing done for a good reason. Our sinful nature's strong side likes to manifest itself through good deeds—giving to the poor, taking people into our home, etc. To be self-aware, we need to examine if we are doing that deed for the wrong reason. Isn't the right thing done with an improper motive still wrong? Matthew 6:1 tells us that Jesus said this: *"Be careful not to practice your righteousness in front of others to be seen by them. If you do, you will have no reward from your Father in heaven."* Even giving without the right motives hinders our prayers: James 4:3 tells us: *"When you ask, you do not receive, because you ask with wrong motives, that you may spend what you get on your pleasures."*

It's important to note that not all motives can be labeled good or bad. We can do things for personal satisfaction, like taking a vacation. We can be motivated to take out the garbage, so it doesn't smell up the house. The important thing is to be self-aware and honest about our motives. Authenticity before God requires asking God to reveal any wrong motives, especially if our deepest desire is for someone to validate or affirm us. This pleases Him as it draws us into a more intimate relationship with Him, as He reveals our reasons, lovingly and gently. When Jesus comes again, 1 Corinthians 4:5 (NIV) says, *"He will bring to light what is hidden in darkness and will expose the motives of the heart. At that time each will receive their praise from God."*

Chapter 15 – The Why

Checking our motives

How do we check our motives? This happens through awareness, examination and honesty.

1) Examine yourself by asking the following questions:

- † What need am I trying to fill by doing this?
- † Would I do this if I knew no one would notice?
- † Would I do this if I knew there would be no return on investment (ROI)?
- † Would I do this if I knew others would misunderstand or question my actions?
- † Does this make me compare myself with others?
- † Am I doing this because someone else is? Or can't?
- † Am I doing this to receive praise from others?
- † Am I trying to impress others?

2) Pray. Ask God to reveal any motives that are not God-honoring. Ask Him to help you become aware and admit your true motives. Admit that you may be doing something just to get noticed. He knows anyway.

3) Check the evidence. Does this activity evidence the fruit of the Spirit? Galatians 5:22-23 tells us: *"The fruit of the Spirit is love; joy; peace; forbearance; kindness; goodness; faithfulness; gentleness, and self-control."*

4) Take notice. Look for ways God satisfies your needs. Look for ways He's already noticing you. Dwelling on our status as a child of God grants mercy to us regardless of our sins. His mercy is freely given, no matter our thoughts or motives.

Application

We can't talk about motivation without talking about judgments. Quite often, we make judgments about others by assuming their motives. We can factually examine an action, like being late. We can say, "You're late." However, it turns into judgment the minute we assume the motive behind it. For example, "You're late because you really didn't want to come to the event."

In the book *How to Stop the Pain*, author James Richards describes it this way: "Although judging has many facets, I believe we all can grasp the most basic and essential aspect, which is this: Identifying what someone did is not judgment; that is merely observation. It is when we assume to know why a person did what he did that we have entered into judgement." A lot of relationships can be preserved when we refrain from committing this kind of "assumicide."

Before we beat ourselves up too much about motives, I want to encourage you. This is the road to self-awareness. Perhaps you rarely consider why you do what you do, but start now. As you use these tools to help you better assess your why, ask God to help you discover your true motives.

Let's get back to the band. I decided to use my own system. As one rehearsal came to an end, my frustrations mounted. As I headed back to my car, those struggling thoughts returned. I proceeded to go through the four steps.

1) I asked myself why I needed to do this and realized that it wasn't to give back. I did it out of fear that there wouldn't be other opportunities.

2) I prayed...and God delivered. He revealed that it wasn't my responsibility to pay back. He is the source of everything I have, so I don't have to strive or pay back anyone.

Chapter 15 – The Why

3) Checking the evidence revealed how my frustrations reflected the flesh, not the Spirit. I was denying myself to prove I was "noble," which only made it worse.

4) I took notice. If I truly believe that God is good, then He knows what is best for me. I learned to trust Him to bring opportunities into my life that honor Him. Could He actually have something else for me to do with the time I was spending at rehearsal? Could this new activity give me that satisfaction that comes only from Him?

My awareness of myself changed that day. My awareness of God changed that day. Friends, He's not holding out on me, and it's okay to wait for Him to deliver! I can say no to things that don't glorify Him, even good things. He notices me—every action, every thought, every motive. And He gives me good things even though I deserve to be punished. Mercy changes everything.

So, instead of being at a rehearsal tonight, I am writing this chapter. And guess what? I'm satisfied.

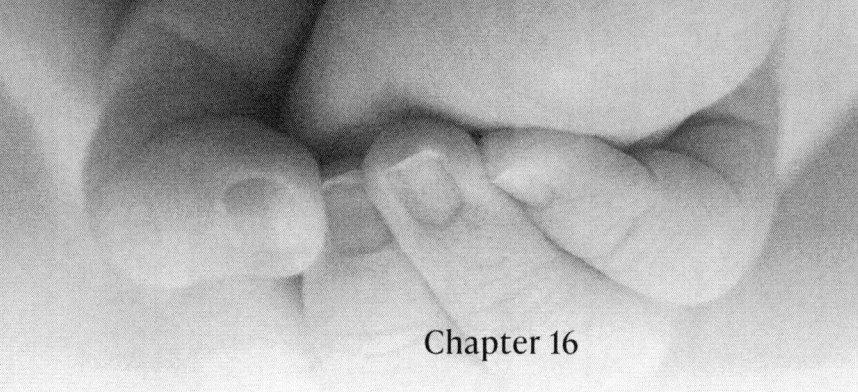

Chapter 16

SELFIES

———————— " ————————

I used to walk into a room full of people and wonder if they liked me...now I look around and wonder if I like them.
—**Anonymous**

Self-love, self-respect, self-worth. I'm amazed they all start with "self." You cannot find them in anyone else.
—**Anonymous**

Niagara Falls is my happy place. Strolling on the meandering trails on the American side, I could hear the water. Awestruck, I stepped closer to the water's edge, my heart pounding with anticipation. With the backdrop of the falls filling my veins, I got distracted by the multiple languages I heard from international tourists taking pictures. And then, I saw them. Not one, not two, but hundreds of the latest tech gadgets…selfie sticks.

Now don't get me wrong. I enjoy a gadget or two. I'm amazed at how technology has shown us new ways of interacting with each other.

I love my phone's camera, videos, and the ease of texting, but taking selfies with selfie sticks? It seemed extreme. Why can't we live in the moment without documenting it?

But that's not the direction our culture is going. Selfies and videos entice us to live in a notice-me world of self-promotion. Social media posts and how many likes or comments we receive have encouraged us to document everything, even the details of our day. Walk down the self-help aisle at a bookstore, and you will see this obsession. Could this be an outcry of an underlying need we all have?

In a recent study regarding the underlying motives behind selfie posts, scholars agreed that two distinct types of personalities emerge. First are narcissists who desire attention. Second are individuals who take pictures for archival reasons. In the quest to be noticed, where do you fall? What is your motive?

Posting items with the motive of self-promotion can have damaging effects, breeding envy. Psychologist Todd Kashdan from George Mason University describes what happens to us when we look at posts. "They're hearing all these great things happening from other people, and they're making a downward comparison to themselves. They're viewing themselves as 'My life isn't as interesting or satisfying as other people's lives look like,' he explained.

Selfies encourage more selfies, and our economy is benefitting. With the pandemic and increasing Zoom calls, we have to buy the right lighting, backdrops, and microphones. I've never looked at myself as much as after a day's worth of Zoom meetings!

This obsession with self doesn't stop there. Take a closer look at the "selfs" listed below.

Chapter 16 – Selfies

The "selfs" (Definitions based on Webster's Dictionary)

† **Self-actualization** | The top tier of Mazlow's Hierarchy of Needs showcases the achievement of our full potential through creativity or independence.

† **Self-absorption** | Focused on getting our needs met, we cannot see that others may have needs.

† **Self-aware** | To be self-aware means you have conscious knowledge of your character, feelings, motives, and desires.

† **Self-care** | Actions an individual may take to reach optimal physical and mental health

† **Self-centered** | Pre-occupation with oneself

† **Self-condemnation** | Blaming oneself

† **Self-confidence** | Confidence in one's powers and capabilities

† **Self-control** | The ability to regulate one's emotions, thoughts, and behavior in the face of temptations and impulses

† **Self-deception** | When we think we're something we're not

† **Self-deprecating** | Being overly modest or critical of oneself

† **Self-effacing** | Not claiming attention for oneself

† **Self-esteem** | Confidence in one's worth or abilities

† **Self-fulfillment** | Realizing one's deepest desires and capacities

† **Self-gratification** | The indulgence or satisfaction of one's desires

† **Self-growth** | Progressive development of self

- † **Self-help** | Use of one's efforts and resources to achieve things without relying on others
- † **Self-image** | The concept one has of their abilities, appearance, and personality
- † **Self-indulgent** | Catering to our desires, passions, and whims without restraint
- † **Self-justification** | The act of justifying oneself, offering excessive reasons or explanations
- † **Self-love** | Regard for one's well-being and happiness
- † **Self-pity** | Extreme, self-absorbed unhappiness over one's troubles
- † **Self-promotion** | The action of promoting or publicizing oneself or one's activities, especially in a forceful way
- † **Self-respect** | Proper respect for oneself as a human being
- † **Self-righteousness** | Confidence in one's righteousness, especially in comparison with the actions and beliefs of others
- † **Self-worth** | The sense of one's value or worth as a person

Relationship with self

Phew. That's a lot of self. I guarantee I haven't mentioned every "self" out there. Our culture and marketplace appeal to all these "selves." But what does the Bible say about self? Two distinct passages come to mind.

Luke 9:23-24 says, *"And he said to all, 'If anyone would come after me, let him deny himself and take up his cross daily and follow me. For whoever would save his life will lose it, but whoever loses his life for my sake will save it.'"* This passage implies that to live life to the fullest,

Chapter 16 – Selfies

we must deny ourselves. Indeed, at salvation, we make that proclamation when we decide we cannot save ourselves. Acknowledgment of our sins and being incapable of saving ourselves is the first step towards denying self.

Yet, as we work through our salvation with fear and trembling, we continue to struggle. This struggle becomes our transformation story but remember, God is the one orchestrating your transformation. He wants us transformed so we can bring His story to others. This is where our dross rises to the surface, and we are cleansed and purified to shine for Him. Yet how can we see the need in others if we can't see it in ourselves?

In my lay counseling sessions, the question of self-denial, selfishness, and self-care often comes up. If I don't choose to serve another because I need to practice self-care, am I denying self? Am I being selfish? Maybe, maybe not. The Word of God doesn't provide us with solutions for every potential scenario. As we become self-aware and stay filled with the Holy Spirit, we will receive discernment. There are plenty of examples where Jesus took care of His physical needs, like rest, thirst, and time alone with God. Denying self doesn't mean denying our humanity. But it does not mean being obsessed with ourselves either.

The second passage that comes to mind, we've talked about already in Luke 10:27, *"You shall love the Lord your God with all your heart and with all your soul and with all your strength and with all your mind, and your neighbor as **yourself**."* Here, Jesus is identifying three distinct relationships: 1) relationship with God, 2) relationship with others, and 3) relationship with self.

As self-aware believers taking more notice of what God is doing, we are more aware of how we may come across to others, and open to the ways we take things personally. If we've told our story and have been validated, we no longer have a need to have others affirm it.

By being aware of the dross in our life, we can better characterize when a conflict is about us or perhaps the other person. By accepting our unworthiness and embracing mercy, we are free to concentrate on offering others the same. We no longer have as many needs as we once did. We forget what is behind because we no longer expect the affirmation of others. The key to achieving balance appears to be accomplished in setting priorities. Love God, first. But the passage continues with a second command. Love your neighbor as yourself.

As yourself

Honestly, the as yourself part of the verse puzzled me for the longest time. Was God saying we should love ourselves? Was this about self-esteem or self-worth? Or was this another way of explaining the Golden Rule from Matthew 7:12: *"So whatever you wish that others would do to you, also do to them, for this is the Law of the Prophets?"*

Treating another the way we'd like them to treat us is a great model. Unfortunately, this isn't always possible. Someone may need something from us that we don't have to give or are experiencing something we've never experienced. Wouldn't it be presumptuous to think we can completely understand what someone needs?

I would argue that "as yourself" could be referring to a healthy relationship with oneself, which requires self-awareness. If we are healthy, we can offer that health to others. But that leaves us with this concept of self-love.

John Piper explains this concept well in his article "Self-love and the Christian Counselor's Task" from *Desiring God*. He said, "Self-love may be defined in two ways in relation to such an understanding of human happiness. First, a person can be said to love himself if he is devoted to his own interest. You love yourself in this sense if you desire and strive for your own happiness. It follows from what I said above that all people love themselves in this sense. Since happiness is the fulfillment of one's desires, and all people desire, therefore, all people long to be happy. The implication is that we will naturally love ourselves. We want to be happy. No one has to teach us that… However, not everyone agrees on where or how happiness is to be found. Each person has their own values and desires to pursue the ones he deems highest. In this sense, all people love themselves. I have argued (Christianity Today, August 12, 1977) that this is the kind of self-love Jesus had in mind when he said, "Love your neighbor as yourself." He did not command self-love; he assumed it and made it the measure of neighbor love."

Friends, please read this section carefully because it is the centerpiece of this book.

We cannot fulfill God's mission without living out this command. We cannot execute this command without understanding our relationship with God, others, and self. Our relationship with God ultimately shows us how to love ourselves and others appropriately.

Self-awareness

Jesus didn't command that we love ourselves. He assumed we did. But He did die to save us from ourselves. I'm not highlighting salvation for eternal life as much as salvation from the hurts, habits, and hang-ups of life…the "dross." Which self should we be the most concerned about?

Since this book focuses on validation and affirmation, I would suggest self-awareness is an excellent place to start. Without being aware of yourself, you can't determine what you need saving from or how much of a deficit you have. Without being aware of yourself, you can't assess your motives or your dross. This is more than self-consciousness. This is about positioning ourselves to receive.

We will struggle to love others with the love of God if we haven't received it for ourselves.

In my twenties, I was self-absorbed. During this season of self-discovery, I was trying to figure out who I was outside my family unit. I wanted to focus on exploring the world, building my career, and finding a potential spouse. Since my fan club was defective, I struggled with feeling good about myself. I obsessed over performances and roles I found myself in. I secretly hoped others would applaud or at least notice my awesomeness. When they didn't, I sometimes sulked in self-pity. I was not self-aware enough to realize that I could not serve others' needs if I was looking to them to serve mine.

We all have a self-survival instinct. But do we all have self-awareness? The intensity of how bad or good we feel about ourselves can vary like the wind or vacillate like a seesaw. As we discover more and more our limitations, mistakes, and sins, we learn how much we need mercy. When we are aware enough to offer mercy to ourselves, we understand how to give it to others.

Take notice

As we become more self-aware, we become more aware of others. As we become more aware of God, we become more aware of what God is doing.

A couple of years back, I organized an event at our church called "The Notice—God Stories Live!" The purpose of the event is to give others the chance to tell their stories. Telling our God stories is a great way to satisfy all three of our relationships. By focusing on what God is doing, whether it's how God noticed us in nature, shopping, relationships, trials, sports, music, or trauma, we see salvation in a different light. Once we share our stories, we validate God's role in our lives. Our need to be noticed is satisfied, and when others listen, they are blessed. Scripture says in Psalms 107:9, *"For He satisfies the longing soul, and the hungry soul He fills with good things."*

The focus of my podcast, *The Notice*, is to encourage us to take notice of what God is doing in both the small and big ways. As we do that, we can remember the many layers of salvation God provides. But let's be honest. The God of the universe doesn't have to do anything for us. Yet, Lamentations 3:22-23 says, *"The steadfast love of the Lord never ceases; His mercies are new every morning; Great is your faithfulness."*

How does God notice us?

Each breath we take is an indication that He notices us. When I was at Niagara Falls, I became more aware of how God noticed me. After I stopped looking at the selfie-sticks, a quiet section near the falls opened up, and tourists moved on. As I closed my eyes and listened, I remembered how much I love the sound of waterfalls. Understanding He noticed what was important to me, I became more aware of His power and place in my life. This space, this moment, was nothing short of majestic. Surrounded by the incredible sights and sounds of moving water, His power was so overwhelming, I worshiped. The God who knows every hair on my head embraced me. Oh, how He satisfies!

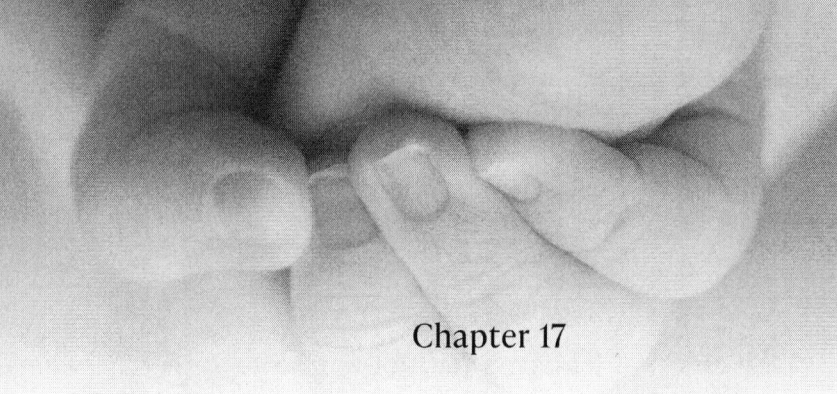

Chapter 17

WHO'S LISTENING?

―――――― " ――――――

Listen and silent are spelled with the same letters.
—Anonymous

French author & Nobel prize winner Andre Gide says, "Everything that needs to be said has already been said. But since no one was listening; everything must be said again."

Stephen Covey says, "People don't listen to understand. They listen to reply. The collective monologue is everyone talking and no one listening."

The thirtieth United States president, Calvin Coolidge, said, "No one ever lost their job by listening too much."

Dr. Ralph Nichols, an expert on the subject of listening and founder of the International Listening Association, says, "The most basic of human needs is the need to understand and be understood. The best way to understand people is to listen to them."

Entrepreneur Jeffrey Fry said: "What is said is not important. What is important is what is heard." A former co-worker of my husband, often said in his Eeyore voice: "Nobody reads. Nobody listens."

So, who's listening? And what does it mean to listen?

The International Listening Association defines listening as "the process of receiving, constructing meaning from and responding to spoken and/or nonverbal messages." As we continue to explore validation and affirmation, we can all recognize that one of the best ways to feel validated is to be heard. Yet many of us struggle to find someone to truly listen.

Science confirms that religious beliefs and a loving, stable community are very healing, providing a place for others to listen, offering psychological benefits. Even to have the chance to say everything out loud to a real person who is actively listening could be all the therapy you need. What happens if our family and friends don't want or don't know how to listen?

Many seek counseling. One in four American adults has visited a counselor at some point in their lives. One in three Christians seek treatment. Bessel Van Der Kolkata, M.D. makes a decisive point in his book, *The Body Keeps Score,* when he writes, "Talking about painful events doesn't necessarily establish community—often, quite the contrary. Families and organizations may reject members who air their dirty laundry; friends and family can lose patience with people who get stuck in their grief or hurt…"

Obviously, there are times when experiencing a considerable loss or life-changing event warrant a counselor's assistance. Placing that level of responsibility onto our loved ones or even our church community may be asking too much. It's also challenging to find the time to listen. As we continue to multi-task, finding the time to sit with someone and hear them out becomes cumbersome.

Empathy

If we actually sit down with someone who will listen, what are we hoping for? Our typical answer is empathy. But as the way we relate to each other socially changes due to technology, we struggle with how to give and receive empathy. In an article written by Dr. Sylvia Hart Frejd in Just Between Us Magazine: *Raising Empathy in a Selfie World"* she said: "In fact, several of the problematic tendencies of our online behavior—comments sections, cyberbullying, and even the 'Facebook envy' we get when we think everyone else's life seems better than ours—can be attributed, at least in part, to a lack of empathy."

Empathy is a vital social skill. When we think of empathy, many of us think of someone who can easily put themselves in our shoes. Empaths are highly sensitive individuals who have a keen ability to sense what other people around them are thinking or feeling. However, not everyone is an empath.

Often, in order to receive empathy, we like to join others going through the same things, especially if it is in the same season of life. Support groups can be a great way to get that kind of empathy. However, we need to take in account that no two people have the same exact experiences. No two people have the same expectations. Instead, what if we could listen long enough to allow the person to share their experience without judgment? Perhaps we can be better listeners by merely acknowledging someone else's experience.

Throughout my lay counseling experience, I have learned how important it is to validate. In fact, I would argue that it is one of the most important listening skills we have. However, we can get into trouble when our expectations for our listeners are unrealistic. I recall the time I said to my husband, "I don't feel like I'm being heard," to which he replied, "I heard you. I just don't agree." If indeed validation is acknowledgement, he was truly acknowledging me. However, what

I was looking for was agreement. It is unfair to accuse someone of not listening just because they don't agree.

As I took a deeper step into my own self-awareness, I discovered eight different listening styles. I define them as characters. As you read this list, it may remind you of a time you didn't feel heard or a time you didn't listen. Perhaps, like me, it may help you become more aware of your own listening style.

Eight "Empathetic" Listening Styles

1) The storytellers. The minute you share your story, the storyteller believes they are being empathetic when they share a similar experience in return. When this happens, you may not feel heard because it seems as though your experience has turned into being all about them.

2) The advisors are quick to tell you how you should respond or what you should do while you are sharing your story. Or even better, what they would do if it were them. Unsought advice could come across as judgment. If someone is giving their opinion, you will not feel as though you have been heard.

3) The judges use blanket statements or platitudes. They typically use blanket responses like "All men are jerks," or a platitude like "Everyone has problems." This may make you feel like your experience is being dismissed.

4) The intruders talk over you or interrupt as you share your experience. They are quick to jump to conclusions without hearing the details. Obviously, you may not feel heard when you can't finish your story.

5) The problem solvers don't necessarily give advice; they just want the problem to go away. Often impatient, they want to jump to a quick solution. Often, when a problem solver tries to solve your problems, you feel like they are trying to control how you should respond. This makes you want to stop sharing.

6) The teachers believe life is a lesson and whatever you are experiencing is a teachable moment. Although you may receive wisdom from them, you feel like you're being corrected or punished when they start to teach.

7) The cheerleader believes they are encouraging you by saying "You've got this" or by trying to make yourself feel better about the situation. You don't feel heard because you feel like they are trying to talk you out of your feelings.

8) The multi-taskers assure you they are listening while actually trying to accomplish two or three things at once. They may be cooking dinner or checking their text messages and promise you they are listening. Obviously, you don't feel heard if your listener is not giving you undivided attention.

New responses

I don't know about you, but going through this list of characters, led me to draw the conclusion that I must be the worst listener alive. Maybe you are guilty of these too. It's not that we should never offer advice, teach, problem-solve, or cheerlead, it's typically just a matter of when. The bottom line is this: Others feel heard when their experience is validated first.

How do we acknowledge? By reflecting back what was heard, especially the feelings someone expressed. A good listener will wait to offer advice. It's all about timing and respect of where the person is at.

Acknowledging someone doesn't mean we approve, condone, or even empathize. Validation supports God's establishment principle of divine space and free will. This means everyone has a right to their perspective and what choices they make, regardless of whether we agree with them or not. While someone might not feel heard because the listener isn't agreeing with their viewpoint, validation isn't agreement. Affirmation includes approval.

What's the best way to acknowledge others so they feel heard? Here are a few different strategies to consider when listening.

1) **Be present**. When listeners are present physically, spatially, and emotionally, they convey to the speaker their experience is worthy of notice. When we're present, we respect the presence, or divine space, of others.

2) **Ask questions**. It's okay for listeners to ask questions as long as they ask permission to do so after they acknowledge. Otherwise, the speaker may respond defensively. A good listener will clarify their questions to help them better understand what they've heard.

It's important to remember that not all people can easily communicate their experiences verbally. Sometimes, people are talking out loud about their experiences because they are trying to help themselves figure out what happened. In such cases, questions can be invaluable to the listener.

3) **Observe body language**. People feel heard and noticed when listeners pick up on their body language. A listener can often learn more from a person's body language than from what is actually said. Mirroring is a great method.

4) **Reflection is validation at its finest.** When someone shares an experience, a good listener will wait until the speaker is finished and respond by reflecting what was said. Reflecting doesn't mean we offer commentary. The listener tries to phrase it differently, highlighting the main point of what was heard. One good characteristic of Zoom meetings is that you can't talk over each other.

5) **Offer a gesture**. I vividly remember an encounter I had when I was going through my divorce. At the time, I was emotionally

exhausted. I couldn't say much because I was sad. One night, as I walked into our Life Group, I collapsed on the couch. Without saying a word, a woman in the group sat down next to me on the couch and began stroking my hair. No words were spoken. It was one of the most meaningful gestures I've received. I felt cared for and loved. Gestures are part of being present. Go ahead and offer a Kleenex because the speaker is crying or provide a glass of water if someone is coughing. A gesture isn't a gesture if you talk about it.

6) **Show mercy**. As believers in Jesus Christ, the most important way to listen is through the eyes of mercy. It doesn't matter what is being shared—even if it is a bad choice or something that negatively affects the listener. Realizing how close we all are to falling makes it easier to show mercy.

What are we saying?

I can't really talk about listening without bringing up an important point: What is it we're really asking others to listen to? Complaints? Gossip? Venting?

During one season of my life, I held an intense job that demanded sixty hours of my life each week. With my work-life balance way off, I found myself being irritable and having an intense need to vent. Naturally, my husband was the one who got to hear my ramblings. He was very patient with me, but I always had more to say. I finally became aware of what I was doing.

During this season of our marriage, my husband and I worked in different cities during the week and would come together on the weekend. After months of this schedule, I began to recognize a destructive pattern. Once he arrived, I vented, and he listened. Sometimes this turned into a long session. God gently showed me this wasn't the best use of our time together.

The next Friday, after he arrived and settled in, it was our time to reconnect. Since our time together often started with venting, I decided this time was going to be different. I decided to limit my venting time by using a timer and setting it for twenty minutes. Twenty minutes went by fast, but I did make myself stop when the timer went off. As the weekend went on, I found myself wanting to vent again, but stopped myself. Instead, I mentally vented to God. This exercise taught me to discipline my thoughts, be more concise about what I needed to share, and recognize that God is the best person with whom to lament.

God is available twenty-four-seven, knows all the details surrounding my work-life intimately, and has the power to do something about my situation. I also discovered that though my husband is a good listener, God sees all and is always listening to His children. Jeremiah 33:3 says, *"Call to me and I will answer you, and will tell you great and hidden things that you have not known."* Psalm 18:6 tells us, *"In my distress I called upon the* Lord*; to my God I cried for help. From his temple he heard my voice, and my cry to him reached his ears."*

God sees the thoughts and intents of my heart and knows my every motive, but He also wants me to dwell on good things instead of what I cannot control. Maybe He doesn't want me to dwell on the negative. Philippians 4:8 admonishes, *"Finally, brothers, whatever is true, whatever is honorable, whatever is just, whatever is pure, whatever is lovely, whatever is commendable, if there is any excellence, if there is anything worthy of praise, think about these things."*

Behind the eyes

It was a beautiful, sunny afternoon, and I wanted to take my dog for a walk. As I approached the park, I noticed that someone had parked their car close to the entrance once again. *How inconsiderate,* I thought. *What gives them the right to park there?* There was barely room for other vehicles to pass. I couldn't believe this person would inconvenience all of us. I was so bothered by it that I peeked inside the car looking for clues about who this person could be. And, of course, I couldn't keep from mentioning this person's rudeness to others.

As I continued my walk, I saw an elderly woman walking with a cane. I remembered seeing her before walking her little dog. As she walked to a park bench to rest, I noticed that her dog wasn't with her. As I passed by the bench, I stopped to visit. After she pet my dog, I asked about hers. Tears immediately came rolling down her face as she explained her dog had died. She explained how the dog meant everything to her and, at her age, he was all she had left to love. As I listened to her story, I couldn't help but empathize with her. As she got up to leave, I asked if I could walk her back to her car.

As we approached her car, I gasped. You guessed it. Her car was *that* car…the one parked close to the entrance. I felt awful. I had judged her out of ignorance. I didn't know her back story. Someday, when I'm old and feeble and taking my beloved dog to the park, I hope that others will show me mercy when I park so close to the entrance. Friends, we don't always know what someone else is experiencing. We don't always know their back story. We need to see behind the eyes and be ready to offer mercy instead.

Mercy sends the message that no one is better than another. We all have limits, make mistakes, and sin. Through mercy, we can give others the benefit of the doubt. May we view effective listening as a gateway to mercy.

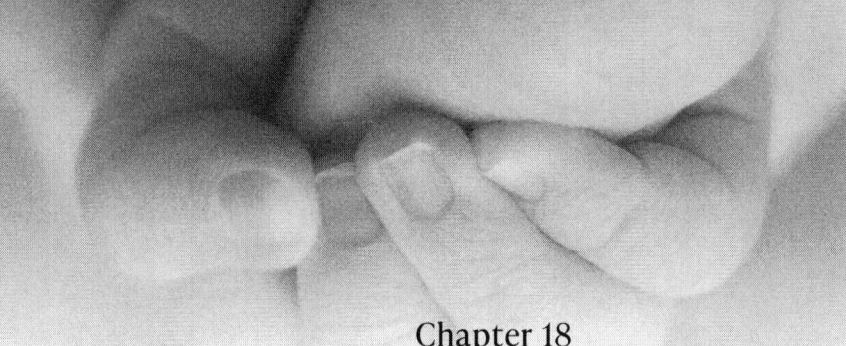

Chapter 18

TREAT YOURSELF

❝

The foolish man seeks happiness in the distance.
The wise grows it under his feet.
— **James Oppenheim**

A sense of deservedness or entitlement will
keep us from knowing Christ.
—**John Piper**

Blessed are the merciful, for they shall receive mercy.
—**Matthew 5:7**

One of the most famous episodes from the TV show "Parks and Rec" is the episode titled *Treat Yo'self*. This episode comically describes how to treat ourselves, whether buying food we like, clothes, massages, vacations, or other ways to be kind to ourselves. We need to not only take care of ourselves, but also indulge. After all, we deserve it.

Self-care is a healthy choice for us to reach our physical and mental health. The marketplace of self-care is ever rising. In Shayla Love's article in "Vice" magazine's Burnout and Escapism issue, she talks about self-care. "There's a whole marketplace of self-care items capitalizing on our distress: self-care makeup, self-care manicures, self-care face masks, self-care massages, self-care detox tea. An article about self-care in *The New Yorker* noted that you can now buy self-care planners and self-care temporary tattoos in the shape of Band-Aids bearing reassurances like 'This too shall pass' and 'I am enough.' These activities and products are not sinister in and of themselves. I would hope that a balanced life includes leisure, time with loved ones, and exercise. But self-care has been appropriated by companies and turned into a kind of tease about the healthcare we should be desperate for. You cannot treat an anxiety disorder with a bubble bath or a meditation app, and the supposition that you can is a dangerous one. If we lived in a world in which we were properly taken care of, would self-care have the same appeal? Is self-care a symbol of a generation that wants to take care of itself, or does it reveal how our society has failed to take care of us?"

It appears the self-care industry pushes us towards self-indulgence by assuming one big thing: we deserve it. On Oprah's final episode of her hugely popular TV show, she talked about deserving our space. She highlighted the importance of validation by saying, "I've talked to nearly 30,000 people on this show, and all 30,000 had one thing in common—they all wanted validation. They want to know. Do you hear me? Do you see me? Does what I say mean anything to you?"

Perhaps Oprah was famous because she understood that all of us, on some level, feel unworthy. By providing a sanctuary for people to share dysfunction in their life, the show provided us with an overall message: Life is tough, but we all deserve a safe place to share our experiences. In other words, if you occupy space, you are worthy. She took it further when she preached that happiness can be found within ourselves. We just have to take responsibility. So, I would say she would probably say: Yes, go ahead and treat yourself. You deserve it.

However, the questions Oprah didn't tackle still linger. Are we worthy? Are we the source of our own happiness? What do we deserve? Using words like deserve or worthiness about our most profound nature carries assumptions. One big assumption is that we are entitled.

Entitlement

Entitlement is a belief that we inherently deserve privileges or special treatment. Entitlement says we don't have to do anything to earn it or deserve it. According to Oprah, all we have to do is exist. If you don't think you're feeling entitled, ask yourself these questions:

- † I deserve to have children, so why can't I get pregnant? After all, aren't children a blessing from God?
- † I'm such a hard worker; why can't I find a higher paying job?
- † I can sing better than her; I deserve to be on the worship team. Why wouldn't God want to use my talents?
- † I'm tired of being single. I've remained pure and focused on Christ. Where is the spouse I've prayed for?
- † I've invested years raising my children, and I've been a great mom. Why don't they call me?
- † I go out of my way to clean the house; I deserve to have a more beautiful home.

† I work hard all day to provide for my family; I deserve to watch TV when I get home.

† I've been so good with my finances; I deserve to buy anything I want.

† I've been disciplined on my diet all week; I deserve to reward myself with this cookie.

Some say this generation is the entitled generation. Frankly, I'm not sure that's unique to this generation. After all, my parents' generation emphasized entitlement too, but in a different way—through the American work ethic. They informed us that if we work hard enough, we will live the dream. Or, better yet, we can achieve whatever we want because we live in a free country. But is that true? Do I have the talent or resources for what I want just because I desire something? Or do I have limits? They sold us on the American Dream: The more we work, the more we get what we deserve.

Ironically, millennials and Gen X's and Z's have trouble seeing it that way. They've watched companies downsize and lay off workers, forcing their parents to change jobs frequently. The stress of moving, juggling two-income families, and lack of extended community contribute to divorce statistics. They don't always see that hard work pays off. Some millennials envision someone walking into a coffee shop they frequent and offering them a high paying job, just because they need it. Or they envision going viral overnight with the latest next thing. Perhaps that's why many of our youth are struggling.

Unfortunately, it's not just our youth who struggle. I have witnessed mid-life adults who are still trying to find their place in the world. They are stuck in jobs they don't love or looking for jobs they deserve. Striving to gain approval in the workplace, they work extra hours, without results. In a quest to prove themselves, they may end up sabotaging themselves from achieving their potential, professionally, relationally, and spiritually. If they don't feel worthy, it may be due to the lack of validation from their fan club. Most often, it was Dad who didn't validate or affirm them. Without that attention, they end up with what experts call 'The Father Wound'.

Wounds

Many of us were neglected, abandoned, or ignored by our fathers. In a Focus on the Family article, *Understanding and healing the father wound*, Alfred C.W. Davis talks about the father wound: "We all come into the world helpless, dependent and needing acceptance, to be treated as worthy, and to be blessed. The father wound is the absence of this love from your birth father."

Have you experienced that wound? Did your father neglect, abuse, or withhold validation? Have you admitted this wound exists or have you ignored it? Becoming self-aware of our wound allows the dross to rise to the surface for cleansing. Our view of our earthly father significantly corresponds to our picture of our heavenly Father.

What Oprah did well was to expose wounds for what they are. She brought dysfunction, including the father wound, out in the open. When truth comes to light, it does bring a sense of relief. Acknowledging the wound is the first step. Then the real work begins. As we become more self-aware, we recognize we may have responded in unhealthy ways to these wounds. As we've discussed in previous chapters, we may end up performing or self-medicating by numbing the wound. We may ignore it or "treat ourselves" as if that is the remedy. If we don't receive that validation we need, we may decide to validate ourselves through self-indulgence, because after all, we deserved it. But wounds still need healing.

The biggest wound

We want to believe we deserve good things. When someone experiences something good, like a new car, we often respond by saying they "deserve it." This cements the idea that by being good people who believe God is good, means we get good things. However, if we're bad, we deserve punishment. Ironically, during seasons of suffering, we shout, "I don't deserve this!" Of course, we'd rather believe we are worthy. But are we? Don't we deserve the wrath of God because of our sinful state?

Contrary to what many say, we aren't born good. Although we are born vulnerable, that doesn't make us innocent. I remember seeing the rebellion in my nine-month-old daughter when she would not lie still while I changed her diaper. I assure you, no one taught her to rebel! Our sin nature is ready to go from day one. The enemy also tempts us through our limitations and mistakes. If we're always messing up, can we honestly say that we deserve anything? Aren't we essentially unworthy?

It doesn't feel good to feel bad. I get it. Instead of accepting unworthiness as inevitable, we look to others to tell us good things and choose people and situations that make us feel better about ourselves. Essentially, the biggest wound is our feelings of unworthiness, of not being good enough.

In Job 34, we get a glimpse of this wound. Job's friend, Elihu, comes to visit and goes on a rant about how God responds to what we do, giving us what our conduct deserves—both good and bad. He implies that somehow Job must have committed some big sin that caused all his suffering. The Law tries to frame our salvation that way. I would conclude Elihu wasn't part of Job's fan club. No validation or affirmation there. Instead, he tried to convince Job that some secret sin in his life affected what God did. Do we really believe we have that kind of power?

Friends, we can't forget God is God. God can do what He wants, when, and how He wants. As the supreme judge, He decides what we deserve or don't deserve. Go ahead and compare yourself with the matchless perfection and holiness of God. We can only conclude we are sinners, making us unworthy. Yet, despite our unworthiness, God provides and blesses. This is based on His character, not our worthiness. Israel experienced provision when God selected them out of all the nations to be His chosen people. Job experienced blessings before and after Satan tested him. Every day, we experience mercy when we go to work, have a roof over our head, or wake up and find ourselves still breathing.

Acknowledge, accept, grasp

Maybe all this talk of being undeserving can make your head hurt. If we let it, we can dwell on what is wrong with us, cramping the mission. Or we can strive to prove to others that we are deserving. Make no mistake. None of us can meet God's standards. What kind of freedom could we experience if we weren't preoccupied with this nagging feeling of unworthiness?

If we could be healed from our father wound, our struggle with our sexuality, or the sins of others, what would our lives look like? Would we notice the irony of sin? Or would we start comparing our sins with others? Friends, we need to acknowledge that sin exists—in us, and in others. You sin. Your parents sin. Your spouse sins. Your co-workers sin. Your pastor sins. We even respond sinfully to others' sins. Why does sin surprise us? Why are we afraid to call it what it is?

Today, even our churches are straying more and more away from the truth of our unworthiness. Most look at church as a place to feel accepted, validated, and affirmed. And because of mercy, we are. But as we look to the church to satisfy this need, are we being realistic? What if they don't accept the unique gifts

I have to offer? What if they challenge me? What if they point out an error in my thinking? Does this make church an unsafe place? Some call Consumer Christianity the same as "treating ourselves." When we have a mindset of getting what we deserve from our churches, we may miss the healing that comes from acknowledging our wounds.

Which leaves us with an overall question: If the church isn't the place to make us feel better about ourselves, how do we transcend this feeling of unworthiness?

Friends, there is only one solution. Acceptance. Accept that you are unworthy. Admit your limitations, your mistakes, your sin and your sinful responses to sin. Accept that we are worthy of punishment. Get comfortable with this being part of our identity without forgetting one crucial, conclusion: it's not the whole story.

When we accept the mercy of God, we realize how profound and simple His message is. By accepting forgiveness, we humbly agree with God that something is wrong with us. But we also receive the gift—not because we did anything to deserve it, but because God is the ultimate judge of what is good and evil. The substitution of Jesus satisfies God's standard of holiness. A standard we cannot achieve. But this acceptance means our feelings of unworthiness are no longer an issue.

For example, the New Testament calls us to turn the other cheek, to not render evil for evil. This level of forgiveness is calling for behavior that mirrors the work of God in Christ. We cannot accomplish this on our own. As sinners, we can't offer forgiveness, because we aren't the source of forgiveness. We can't even forgive ourselves. Instead, by *accepting* God's mercy for ourselves, we obtain *His* forgiveness, which allows us to extend it to others.

Remember the Message Default System we discussed previously? As we grow in mercy, we don't default to those messy messages.

Instead, we default to a new system: The Mercy Response System. (MRS) This system reminds us that Christ has freed us from this craving for validation. This system relinquishes revenge because we know we are so close to falling ourselves. We can stop looking to exalt ourselves or squash others because of their sin. We are no longer surprised by sin. Instead, we become surprised by mercy.

Does embracing mercy mean we deny ourselves? I'm not saying that we don't treat ourselves at all. We begin to live with an awareness that we don't have to seek excess pleasure to numb our feelings of unworthiness. We don't repair our frame by entering the Hall of Shame or finding ways to treat ourselves because no one acknowledges how sin has affected our lives.

Mark Galli, in his article, "What We Deserve," explains mercy this way: "When Jesus says blessed are the merciful, for they shall receive mercy, He assumes that you really can't be merciful until you've received mercy in the first place. Mercy is not a deal but an ongoing lifestyle. We receive mercy, then we show mercy, and as a result, we receive more mercy, and as a result, we then show more mercy—and on and on. It's like we're rolling a snowball downhill. We start with a small one, maybe the size of a baseball. As we toss it down the hill, immediately gravity starts to pull it farther downhill. As it rolls over, of course, it collects more snow. Now it's bigger and heavier, and so gravity pulls it even harder. It rolls over even faster, and collects more snow, and gets heavier, and rolls faster. And so on. Before you know it, it's a huge ball, bounding down the hill. That's how it is with mercy: The more we receive mercy, the more we give mercy."

Kristen Wetherall in her article *"You Don't Want What You Actually Deserve,"* explains, "If we want to call God's judgment for sin undeserved, then what should we call His gospel? Isn't the good news that God's perfectly Holy Son bore God's wrath completely unmerited in our place? Isn't the gift of His righteousness in exchange for our sin just that—a gift? Yes, and praise God for this! In Jesus, we're given what we do not deserve, so we'll never get what we do deserve apart from Him."

So how can you authentically treat yourself? A trip to the spa, a sunny vacation, a massage or a new outfit will satisfy only temporarily. The ultimate treatment is mercy. Replacing your Message Default System (MDS) with the Mercy Response System (MRS) can happen in three steps: acknowledge, accept, and grasp.

Acknowledge that you have human limitations, you make mistakes, and that there *is* something wrong with you—sin. Acknowledge that there is something wrong with everyone else—sin. Acknowledge that you have looked for ways to numb yourself, make vows, bury yourself in shame, treat yourself, and cramp the mission.

Accept that you are unworthy, and that is okay. Accept your defective fan club, frame, or that those closet to you cannot wholly satisfy this deep, inner need that says you're not good enough. That's why you need the validation and affirmation which comes from mercy.

Grasp onto God's mercy. Mercy tells you that what is wrong with you or your feelings about what is wrong with you are no longer an issue! Grasp that God's mercy is the ultimate validation and affirmation. Grasp a life where you don't ruminate about what is wrong with you. Grasp mercy. Gain confidence.

Let's take it further and learn to live in Mercy Mode.

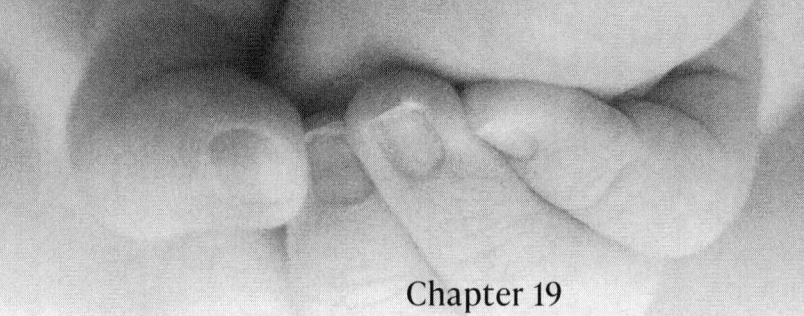

Chapter 19

MERCY MODE

"

We spend so much time creating a façade of what we want to project to the world; we almost forget what we ourselves are truly about in the process.
— **Jason R. Thrift**, *The Civilization Loop: The End Is the Beginning*

Until we taste the bitterness of our own misery, we will never relish the sweetness of God's mercy. Until we see how foul our sins have made us, we will never pay our tribute of praise to Christ for washing us...If you would know the heart of your sin, then you must know the sins of your heart!
—**William Secker**

Growing up in a low socio-economic Detroit community in the late 1970s wasn't easy. Segregation was the latest trend, and the school I attended in Detroit brought students in by bus from across the city. As a result, our neighborhood turned over quickly. During ninth grade, our school was seventy percent white and thirty percent black. By the time I graduated four years later, the percentages reversed—twenty percent white and eighty percent black.

At football or basketball games, the police escorted the band out at halftime because there were fights at the end of the games. A white girl with long hair did not dare go to the bathroom alone at school since it was common to be attacked and have her hair cut off. In between classes one day, a gang member pulled a knife on me. Weeks later, I was beaten up by some girls who just wanted to "play with the snow." I remember that feeling in the pit of my stomach when I heard a girl got shot in our cafeteria. Police, not security guards, were always present, and gates and bars lined every hallway. Going to prom wasn't a safe option either.

However, as I look back on my time in high school, I learned a lot. One could say that I gained street smarts, but I also discovered how to be responsible for my education. Our school boasted many talented and dedicated teachers who prepared us for college.

High school is rarely about classes. Friends, dating, sports, extra-curricular activities, and social life were more important. For me, it was the band. I loved music, enjoyed practicing, and our band director was amazing. A talented, loyal prankster, he had the ability to make you feel like you were the only one in the room. He seemed to gravitate to those of us without a father, taking us under his wing. As a result, he became my male role model. I even decided to major in music in college because I wanted to be a band director just like him.

One afternoon this man of color asked to see me in his office. You weren't called to his office unless you were in some of kind of trouble, so I nervously entered. He explained that the school principal was investigating my report regarding being beaten up by the girls "playing with the snow." I guess the principal wanted to see if I was the kind of person who would lie about something like that.

Chapter 19 – Mercy Mode

Once I came to peace that his questions were motivated by him doing his job, I began to notice something else. He acknowledged me. He acknowledged how traumatic it must have been for me to be beaten up because I was white. He admitted it was wrong and affirmed me for being brave enough to come forward. He validated AND affirmed my experience.

The next words he spoke were life-changing and still resonate with me today. He said, "I hope you know that you can't live to believe all black people are like that. There are plenty of us living to change that perception. You may think they took away your power, but only temporarily. Most important, you have the power over how you will respond. Aggressiveness and determination are two of the outstanding qualities of your personality—don't let anyone cheat you out of those."

As I received his validation and affirmation, I embraced the power of response. I didn't understand it then, but I can recognize now that he was demonstrating mercy. He was God's gift of mercy to me…a girl without a dad…a girl without a fan club.

Living it out

His display of mercy extended to others as well. He established a different culture in the band room. At the time, bi-racial couples were rare. But for him, there didn't seem to be black or white. Music was our bond, our escape from the serious issues plaguing our school.

One of my white friends began dating a black guy in the band. I never gave it a second thought until I saw her conservative family's adverse reaction to the relationship. They kept reciting the verse about being unequally yoked, but she responded that the verse was referring to a Christian marrying a non-Christian. Since she and the boy were both Christians, she didn't see the problem, but her parents did. Hopelessly in love, they hid their relationship from her parents, which meant sneaking around a lot. When she got pregnant, her family's most deep-rooted fears were realized. They were devastated. An out-of-wedlock, racially mixed grandchild wasn't their plan for their talented daughter.

As the pregnancy continued, the baby's parents were justifiably nervous but also excited about the birth. I watched as my band director came alongside the father to support him and his new responsibility without the appearance of judgment or condemnation. He did more than just encourage their musical talent. He seemed concerned with helping them tackle their new commitment. I didn't recognize it at the time, but I now see he was acting out of mercy.

When I saw him living out mercy, I came up with my own idea. I talked to my mom, and we decided to give my friend a baby shower. Although I disagreed with my friends' choice to be sexually involved so early, it became obvious they were going to keep the baby. I saw a need and filled it.

Honestly, teenagers are often self-absorbed, so it surprises me that I even thought of it. Looking back, I saw how much her parents' response hurt her, and knew she needed support. The day of the shower, we weren't sure her Mom was going to come. At the last minute, her Mom decided to show up. Mercy.

Mercy matters

Mercy has many facets. Yes, it's about helping others but perhaps it's more. In Mathew Schmalz's book, *Mercy Matters: Opening Yourself to the Life-Changing Gift*, he describes mercy as "a love that responds to human need in an unexpected or unmerited way."

A cluster of related words in the Hebrew Bible are often translated as *mercy*, depending upon where they appear in the text. There is *ahavah*, which refers to God's enduring love for Israel, much like the love between a husband and wife. Then there is *rachamim*, which comes from the root word *rechem*, or *womb*, and therefore might be more literally understood as suggesting a maternal connection between God and human beings.

In a famous passage from Psalm 85 that speaks of the Israelites' return from exile, it is said that when *"mercy and truth have met together, righteousness and peace have kissed."* Chesed, the word translated as *mercy* in this verse, additionally suggests God's quality of steadfast loyalty. Thus, the Psalm relates steadfastness and mercy with *truth*—in Hebrew *emet*—which means behaving ethically and being faithful to God's will.

Indeed, Mercy is a response to human need. It is an enduring, passionate love, like the unconditional love of a mother, and is steadfast. But it's even more.

Mercy in the Gospels

A point of connection between the Jewish and Christian traditions is what is called the Great Hallel. *Hallel* means *praise* and refers to a group of psalms regularly recited at the time of the new moon as well as during important Jewish feasts like Tabernacles or Sukkot, which commemorate the period the Jewish people spent in the desert on their journey to the Promised Land.

In Psalm 136, The Great Hallel is the refrain which celebrates how God's mercy endures forever. Some scholars believe Jesus sang the Great Hallel with His disciples when they went out to the Mount of Olives after the Last Supper, the final meal He shared with them before His crucifixion.

Aside from lasting forever, mercy sets the context for many of Jesus' teachings. In Matthew, Jesus tells the story of the unmerciful servant who has his own debt wiped away but refused to forgive another servant who owed him only a few cents. The story teaches us that we need to forgive others, not because we are better than others, but because we have received forgiveness ourselves.

Jesus as the face of mercy

Merriam-Webster dictionary defines mercy as "compassion or forbearance." These words convey a level of condescension. We may think "Aren't I something, helping out this person who's less fortunate than I?" Aren't I taking the high road when I forgive someone else?" Part of the problem is that mercy sounds too much like pity to us.

Jesus never responded to people with that kind of attitude, even though as the sinless Son of God, He was actually stooping to our level. Instead, he placed himself in a position of reaching across the table, of treating each person with respect and dignity.

Matthew Chapter 9, vs. 23, Jesus tells His disciples to process the meaning of the phrase: *"Go and learn what this means: 'I desire mercy, and not sacrifice.' For I came not to call the righteous, but sinners."*

Perhaps most significantly for Christians, Jesus shows us what it means to be merciful: He healed the sick, welcomed the stranger, and pardoned those who persecuted and killed Him.

Yet Jesus longs for us to move beyond the idea of sacrifice. Sacrifice is perceived as religious. Instead, He wants us to get our hearts involved. This means tangling up with other people's lives, their dross, their back story, so the word sacrifice drops out of our vocabulary. Jesus ate with his friends because He wanted to. He didn't do it out of duty.

As Pope Francis tells us in Misericordiae Vultus, his letter introducing the Holy Year of Mercy, Jesus' mercy is not abstract but "visceral"—it's something that quite literally changes us from the inside out. And Christians believe that this visceral aspect of mercy comes in the personal relationship Jesus promises to all of us: a relationship based on forgiveness and love, reconciliation, and truth. As Pope Francis writes in the very first sentence of Misericordiae Vultus, "Jesus Christ is the face of God's mercy."

Mercy gives

We don't go through this journey of awareness—learning about our fan club, discovering traps our frame can cause, and making vows—to no purpose. God intends for a deeper understanding of mercy to heal us. If we haven't received mercy for ourselves, we don't understand it enough to give it away.

The Bible is full of stories of mercy, but the story of the prodigal son is a remarkable display. Jesus had just finished with the Lost Sheep and Lost Coin parables, but He also wanted to address the Pharisees complaint about Him welcoming sinners and even eating with them.

The story begins with a man who had two sons. The rebellious younger son, the rule breaker, was disobedient, obviously lost with visible sins…so much so that he had the nerve to ask for his inheritance early so he could set off on his journey. He ended up spending all his inheritance on wild living; he was penniless, then a severe famine hit. Hitting rock bottom, he took a job feeding pigs—unclean animals Jews were not to touch. He was so hungry, he longed to eat the pigs' food. While living this way, he thought it would be better to be his father's servant than to continue in his current lifestyle. So, he came to his senses and, in humility, decided to return to his father and ask for forgiveness.

Meanwhile, the older brother stayed home and did his duty.

Then the younger son returned, and the father was so excited that he ran to him with joy. He asked his servants to prepare a feast to celebrate his son's triumphant return. When the older son came in from the fields to discover a party complete with food, music, and dancing to celebrate his younger brother's return, he was overcome with jealous anger.

Friends, the father in this story is a picture of our heavenly Father. God is full of compassion and has a heart bent towards reconciliation. He is patient and values lost people. He offers up His kingdom, restoring our relationship with joyful celebration. He doesn't dwell on our frame or our Hall of Shame. He affirms us. He doesn't give a sermon on his son's unworthiness.

The older son is a picture of the Pharisees. In their self-righteousness, they continually compare themselves to others, looking down on them in disgust. His relationship with God and his father was cramped because of his resentment. Mercy is both no respecter of persons and deep respect of persons simultaneously.

What is keeping you from getting a firm grasp on the depths of God's mercy? Will you believe this God of mercy welcomes you no matter how lost you are? Once we surrender our perspective and embrace the possibility that God has a better way, we are safe to open ourselves up to a more intimate relationship with God and deep, satisfying relationships with others.

A few years ago, I had the honor of running into my former band director at a music education seminar. As he shared ways to

Chapter 19 – Mercy Mode

encourage students, I piped up and shared what he had done for me. I was *so* glad I got to thank him personally. A year later, he died. And remember the young couple to whom he showed mercy? Well, they just celebrated their fortieth wedding anniversary!

Mercy lives. Mercy gives. Mercy is the greatest love, so celebrate. Get a firm grasp on your safety net, receive mercy, and get ready. Pick out the favorite colors which reflect your unique facets so you can create your masterpiece. God has a painting for you to paint. Embrace.

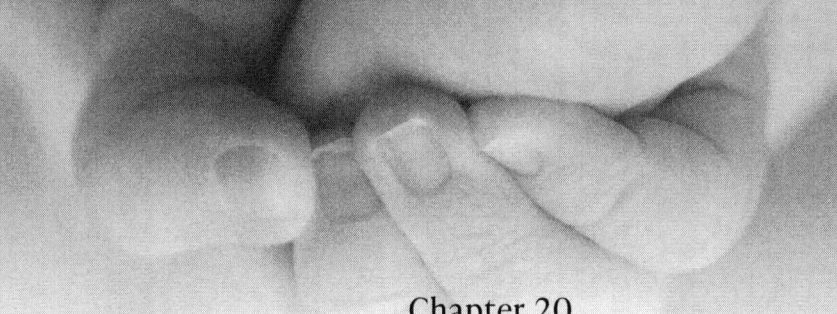

Chapter 20

SAFETY NET

"

Whoever dwells in the shelter of the Most High will rest in the shadow of the Almighty. I will say of the Lord, 'He is my refuge and my fortress, my God, in whom I trust.'
—**Psalm 91:1-2**

He will cover you with his feathers, and under his wings you will find refuge; his faithfulness will be your shield and rampart.
—**Psalm 91:4**

When we go to the circus, we see nets everywhere, catching the acrobats when they fall. In today's notice-me culture, we hear a lot about feeling "safe" or having safety nets. In practical terms, safety nets surround us. For example, unemployment benefits provide a temporary safety net for the unemployed. Those who cannot afford health insurance might get coverage under the safety net of Medicaid. Food stamps are a safety net for those who cannot afford to buy food. Retired people who are no longer earning wages sometimes have the safety net of Social Security. Money in a savings account can be a safety net for unexpected expenses. These safety nets provide for earthly needs.

However, the latest research in neurobiology shows that we also need emotional safety. Safety is crucial to feeling validated and one of the most important aspects of a satisfying connection. If we want to connect best with others, we need to feel safe enough to be vulnerable. Brené Brown reminds us, "Vulnerability is the birthplace of love, belonging, joy, courage, empathy, accountability, and authenticity."

Emotional safety

What is emotional safety? And what does that have to do with validation? Many define emotional safety as unconditional love. Sometimes, we can take it so far that we determine someone is safe if they agree with us. Rarely do we think of emotional safety as being about us.

As we develop self-awareness, it's helpful to acknowledge what we are feeling. If we are secure enough in how we feel, it makes it easier for us to be vulnerable and reveal ourselves to others without worrying about the risk. But we can't do that effectively if we expose something about ourselves that isn't real or true.

For example, if you're tired, but you communicate you are sad, it's likely that others will respond to your sadness, because that's what you identified. But if you're not self-aware enough to realize you are tired instead of sad, you may conclude others haven't validated you, or perhaps we're not emotionally safe. Is it realistic to expect from others what we haven't discovered ourselves?

Friends, emotional safety is so prevalent in our culture that in our expectation, we end up getting easily offended when someone doesn't agree with us. We become quick to accuse others, when in reality, we are the ones not sure of what we're feeling. Not only have

Chapter 20 – Safety Net

we failed to communicate our authentic selves, but our expectations become unrealistic; and we risk the relationship when we're not true to ourselves.

Communicating our needs authentically provides safety to others. In general, we need three things to feel safe. Acceptance and trust in ourselves, acceptance and trust in the other person, and no outside threats. Of these three things, we have control over only one—ourselves.

One of the best ways we can provide safety for others and feel safe ourselves is to acknowledge our thoughts and feelings. Acknowledgment builds trust. By trusting ourselves—including our limitations, motives, mistakes, and sins—we can offer that to others.

Cloud and Townsend, in their book *Safe People*, describe safe relationships this way: "A safe relationship is one that does three things: One, draws us closer to God. Two, draws us closer to others. Three, helps us become the real person God created us to be."

Eyewitness

As we develop safe relationships, acknowledgment starts with taking notice. We need someone to acknowledge our day, what we've gone through, how we feel. But we have to offer the same to the other person. We cannot expect others to read our minds. Enter the eyewitness.

In the movie "*Shall We Dance*," Beverly Clark (played by Susan Sarandon) describes marriage in this way: "We need a witness to our lives. There's a billion people on the planet...I mean, what does anyone's life really mean? But in a marriage, you're promising to care about everything. The good things, the bad things, the terrible things, the mundane things...all of it, all of the time, every day. You're saying 'Your life will not go unnoticed because I will notice it. Your life will not go un-witnessed because I will be your witness.'"

Marriage is one way for us to get our eyewitness needs met. But what if we're single, single again, or an empty nester? How do we build authentic relationships and feel noticed if we don't have an eyewitness?

Authenticity

Satisfying relationships require authenticity. God is the one we can be the most authentic with because He sees our every thought. Brené Brown, who seems to have become our modern-day evangelist for authenticity and vulnerability, states, "Authenticity is the daily practice of letting go of who we think we're supposed to be and embracing who we are."

Doesn't that sound good? Yet, what if we discover we can't embrace who we are? Or we can't figure out what we feel? What if we get stuck on our feelings of unworthiness?

It's not that easy to accept and trust ourselves if we've messed up. As we long to be known and loved as we truly are, including the good, bad, beautiful, and ugly, we often hesitate to reveal the icky parts of ourselves. We want to be seen, but we still want to be respected. By hiding our true feelings, we may hide in our Hall of Shame, only leading to isolation. Ironically, if we isolate ourselves, we become even more lonely, making it even more challenging. If we share, we take a huge risk of being hurt. What will others think if they know the truth?

As we take that into our relationships, we may assume revealing ourselves is setting ourselves up for rejection. The irony is that the very thing that connects us is the very thing we are scared to share. Friends, we all make mistakes, have limitations, and sin. Doesn't that bond us?

Chapter 20 – Safety Net

Storytelling

Finding the right person to share ourselves with requires trial and error. I've opened up at times and later regretted it—not because I wasn't being vulnerable, but because the other person wasn't. Other times, I've shared myself and felt connected. Without self-awareness, we can't identify our story. Sharing our story is one of the best ways to share the message of Jesus.

Friends, you have a story. Someone needs to know about the dross in your life. This is what Jesus saved you from; it is your testimony to His faithfulness. To embrace the mercy of God in our lives, we need to share with others what God has done. We can't let God's testimony of what He's done in our lives be silenced. This is part of our healing!

If you still struggle with your frame, the trap of inadequacy, your why, your identity, or any of the other things discussed in this book, you are not alone. Accept your human limitations, recognize your mistakes and live as if being unworthy is no longer an issue with God. Since God is your ultimate eyewitness, doesn't He already know it anyway? Is there anything that surprises God?

If you're unsure about revealing yourself, think back to the times you have listened to someone else's testimony. I'm sure you've heard stories of illness, divorce, rape, sexual abuse, addictions, and pride. Or perhaps your own story includes being single over fifty, adjusting to an empty nest, or pornography. Maybe you've had a terrible childhood that included abuse, neglect, or just being ignored. The glorious part of any of these stories isn't the dross. The power of story includes acknowledgment and celebration. If no one knows your story, they can't acknowledge it. Without acknowledgement, how can we celebrate what God has done?

My passion for acknowledgement and celebration led me to start a podcast called *The Notice*. The heart behind the podcast is to encourage us to tell stories of God noticing us. If indeed He's the one who knows all and sees all, He is the perfect eyewitness to our lives. In each episode, we take notice of God through stories with special guests or biblical musings. Guests have shared how they noticed God in chronic pain, politics, hoarding, abortion, and creativity, to name a few. I also do a live version called *God Stories Live!* where we offer others the opportunity to share God stories. We've had musicians share songs, a filmmaker shared a film, an actor presented a biblical monologue, and those with addictions and handicaps shared what God has done in their lives. As each person tells their story, they are validated. Others are blessed by hearing what God has done, and a celebration begins. We are reminded yes, redemption wins! Taking notice of what God is doing is contagious. It helps us take more notice of what God is doing!

Storytelling and authenticity is a big deal to Jesus. It brings darkness to the light. In Luke 12:2-3 (MSG), Jesus said, *"You can't keep your true self hidden forever; before long you'll be exposed. You can't hide behind a religious mask forever; sooner or later the mask will slip, and your true face will be known."*

Part of our mission is to tell stories. I want to encourage you to gain enough self-awareness to feel safe enough to share your true self. This includes mistakes, limitations, sins, and responses to sin—the good, the bad, the ugly, the beautiful. Without authenticity and the opportunity to share, we don't receive the validation we need. Instead, we stay in our halls of shame, cramp our lives, or get caught in the trap of inadequacy. We dwell on our frame or look to others to satisfy.

Building a fan club

Who are your safe people? Are you a safe person? Do you have a fan club? If not, I encourage you to start one!

Chapter 20 – Safety Net

A fan club is different than a social club. A fan club includes people who do life with you. They know the ups and downs of what is happening in your life. You are authentic with them, and still, they are your fans. They pray for you and encourage you. They are *for* you. Unfortunately, it takes a while to build a fan club. To feel safe, we have to take the time to share.

However, please be careful. Sometimes, we may select people to be in our fan club based on how they make us feel or what we can gain from them. A fan club isn't a transactional relationship. It's becoming aware of the people God put in your life of whom *you* are a fan.

As we go through different seasons of life, our fan club may change. When we were younger, we may have wanted to be on an athletic team, so we hung out with others who were athletic. Maybe we selected friends with similar interests or a group that could help us meet members of the opposite sex. Sometimes, we may become friends with people who have troubled lives. Taking on their problems can make us feel good about our own lives. Or perhaps we enjoy trying to fix theirs.

As you become aware of your fan club, I urge you to surround yourself with others based on mutual affection. We aren't gathering a fan club for us to be validated. We are gathering a fan club to validate others. Select people you enjoy and would follow. Or consider someone who feels that way about you.

Personally, I have a four-tiered fan club—inner, outer, extended, and members. My inner circle includes the people who regularly connect with me, like my spouse, best friend, counselor, and mentor. My extended family, small group, and close friends are in my outer circle. They know me, but not the play by play. My extended circle includes colleagues, church family, and a larger social circle. They are fans, but at a distance. I may not be as vulnerable with them as I would my inner circle. Lastly, are members. Members are individuals into whom I pour myself. I'm a member of their fan club even though they aren't able to be a member of mine.

It's important to note, that in all of these cases, we can't expect to have fans if we aren't a fan ourselves. Start with the people who are already in your life, the ones with whom you feel safe. Decide which circle they belong to. If you find yourself with only members, you will feel a deficit. I encourage you to build the inner circle first. Find a counselor or mentor to balance the outer circle with the inner circle.

In Christian communities, I admit, it's not always easy. We all know the 'church lady.' It's the woman in the church who thinks she doesn't have any dross, and if you share something with her, everyone in the church suddenly knows. The only way to find safe people is to take a risk. Share something personal, but not too personal, and see what happens. It takes time to feel safe enough to share our innermost struggles.

Small groups can be a great place to build a fan club. When doing life together, your need to be noticed may be satisfied here. You may even satisfy someone else's need. But what happens if you share something and aren't validated? Do you leave the group? Some of us expect so much more from our small group than is intended.

I distinctly remember a time when a person in our small group was vulnerable. He hadn't been coming to group, so I would check in to see how he was doing. For weeks, he said he had to work late. When he finally returned to group weeks later, he admitted to lying to me. He wasn't working late. He just said that because he didn't want anyone to know he was struggling with alcohol again. How beautiful it was when the entire group didn't try to rescue him—but instead, loved on him by validating him for confessing. It's a moment I'll never forget.

For me, being vulnerable meant telling my story, which helped me develop deeper, more loving relationships. Although my story includes physical violence, sexual betrayal, divorce, a deficient fan club, and shame, I wasn't aware of how lost I felt until God provided me with a safe person with whom I could be vulnerable. As I revealed the layers of hurt, I began to see that my perceptions of the world were off. As described in Dan Allender's *The Wounded Heart,* in chapters 5 through 9, there are feelings of powerlessness, betrayal, ambivalence, secondary symptoms, and struggles in relating to others. The inner damages of sexual abuse are huge and need to be walked through carefully. God brought a mentor into my life who became my first safe person. As we met every week to uncover my story, every gruesome detail, I was validated. She watched as God healed me from the past and having her as an eyewitness when my marriage fell apart was a crucial step towards freedom and mercy.

False sense of security

Allow me to offer a word of caution. Although having a fan club is necessary for a full life, we need to be careful. Sometimes, relying strictly on someone else to give validation can give us a false sense of security, like a safety net. Although safety nets are tangible, and we can see them, they can fail. After all, they are designed by humans, manufactured by humans, assembled by humans, so they are not a sure thing. Neither are the humans in our fan club perfect. We need to recognize that others have issues and can't always be ready to be our fan. No person is a hundred percent safe.

A safety net is something we depend on to catch us. Many times, our fan club can catch us when we fall. Anchoring on our fan club as our only safety net isn't foolproof. God offers more. He doesn't just catch us, He *carries* us. He's much more than a safety net, He's our refuge. We aren't promised that there will never be a storm, but God promises shelter when it hits. We aren't promised that others with their limitations, mistakes, and sins won't fail us, but we are promised God's refuge.

As I was going through my divorce, the emotional storm of my life, His shelter was never more needed. When the one person I trusted to be my eyewitness turned out to be the one who betrayed me, I questioned everything and everyone and didn't know who to trust. Although I had a small fan club, they didn't understand me the way God did.

God is our true refuge because, while the earthquakes or the mountains fall, God sits above it all. He alone remains steadfast and secure. He cannot be overwhelmed. He cannot be reduced to trembling. The psalmist says, when the world is falling apart, find security in the God who can never fall apart. Psalms 46:1-3 tells us, *"God is our refuge and strength, a very present help in trouble. Therefore, we will not fear though the earth gives way, though the mountains be moved into the heart of the sea, though its waters roar and foam, though the mountains tremble at its swelling."*

With God as my refuge, I was able to embrace a whole new way of looking at the world. Resting in His safety, I could take risks. I could remain confident in knowing that whatever worst-case scenarios lie ahead, or even when I have a faulty fan club, I can find shelter in Him. Friends, you are safe. Resting in His safety allows us to embrace whatever comes next, no matter how hurtful.

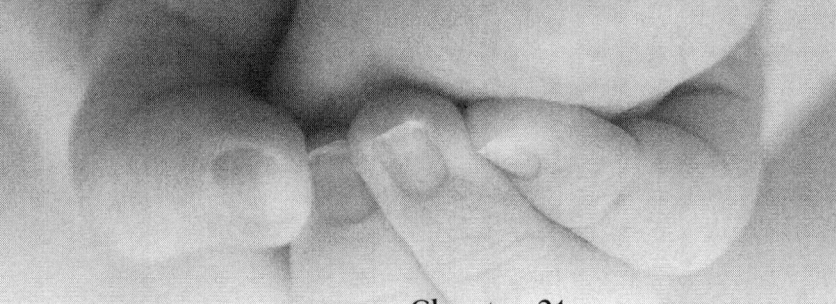

Chapter 21

EMBRACE

———————————— " ————————————

Embracing personal vulnerability is required if you wish to work, plan, and succeed in the future.
—Bill Jensen

It's not about hiding your imperfections on a shoot; it's about embracing them and being unapologetic about them.
—Erin O'Connor

Each day I walk past the full-length mirror on my bedroom wall. Mirrors never felt like friends. In fact, I didn't always own a full-length mirror. My struggles with my weight only solidified this love-hate relationship. Yet, at this time, on this day, something was different. As I walked past the mirror, I heard loud and clear God wanted me to stop and take notice.

As I took a step closer, I didn't like what I saw. Instead of observing my positive features, all I saw was pain etched on my face. I guess my weariness over my pending divorce didn't look so good. As I continued to reflect, my mind began to flood with memories of our twenty-year marriage. How did we get here? How do I respond to rejection? What is God trying to accomplish by having me stare at myself in a mirror?

Romantic notions swirled in my head as I flashbacked to our engagement. As a young adult in my twenties, I was filled with so many hopes and dreams about what our future would look like. Discussions about how many babies we would have, where we would live, and where our careers would take us were filled with hope and expectation. Of course, no one enters marriage thinking it's going to end, but we did discuss divorce and agreed that most divorces happen for one or more of the following reasons: adultery, addiction, or abuse. I never thought I would be faced with any of these scenarios. Instead, here I was, looking in a mirror, all by myself, experiencing an emotional pain so deep, that words escaped me.

I thought back to the exact moment I knew our marriage was in crisis. In the blink of an eye, as I read one line in a letter, my whole world changed. As I read the unexpected details in disbelief, an overwhelming, uncontrollable panic shook my body. Experts label this trauma, but all I could remember was being swallowed up with paranoia. Surely, this can't be happening. Was my whole life a lie? The next thing I remember is frantically dashing out of the house barefoot and running at top speed around our well-manicured sub-division. As I ran out of breath and came to a complete stop, I let out a painful wail. Like glass shattering into little pieces, my heart fell to the ground. Nothing could have prepared me for this.

The intensity of emotions and the seriousness of the decisions which followed left me frightened and anxious. After all, divorce affects an entire community, not just me. Everyone surrounding me had opinions on what I should do based on their experiences, values, and facets. I consulted my pastor, counselors, family, and friends, but it became abundantly clear this was the loneliest decision of my life.

Chapter 21 – Embrace

At first, I chose reconciliation. I didn't want to be divorced and I didn't want my daughters to grow up without a father in the home. Reconciliation turned out to be more difficult than I could ever imagine. Like peeling an onion, layers and layers of forgiveness, psychological issues, and a double life brought more tears. My marriage was in serious trouble, and something needed to change. Someone needed to change. Since I could only change me, I self-examined. Was I too busy? Did he feel unnoticed? Did I fail to affirm him? All this analysis left me numb.

As days turned into weeks, months, and years, I looked for remorse, validation, affirmation, and repentance, but it didn't come. As I took responsibility for the majority of the problems in our marriage, I learned about boundaries, self-awareness, and what it means to enable. After ten years of working through these layers, the outward symptoms improved, but deep-rooted struggles resurfaced. No wonder I could only see weariness on my face.

My dear readers, facing rejection hurts to the core. It's a pain so personal, I wouldn't wish it on my worst enemy. Imagine me curled up in a fetal position, moaning. Envision me so numb I became paralyzed, struggling to make decisions. All I could do was draw this conclusion: something must be wrong with me.

Wrestling with unworthiness was exhausting. It seems when challenging times come, I tend to look for others to validate me, go into problem solving mode, or retreat. Eventually, I discover my helplessness and turn to God. This time, there was no choice but to surrender.

It's amazing what happens when you give in. Although God is always there, somehow, I suddenly notice Him showing up. The first thing God did was bring a woman into my life to disciple me. Authentically, week after week, we met at a local diner. She patiently listened to the details of my failing marriage, unfulfilled dreams, and resentment towards God. She helped me become aware of my frame and comforted me when the dross of my life rose to the surface. As I participated in various healing programs, God gently changed the way I thought about myself and others. For the very first time, I felt validated. I felt heard. I felt seen. Friends, this is what happens when God brings darkness to the light.

Although I grew spiritually, I struggled socially. At church, no one knew what to say to me. I felt like a virus no one wanted to catch. At work, others seemed more concerned with productivity and avoided discussing anything personal. Friends and family were well meaning but didn't want to take sides. The biggest surprise was when on top of all this turmoil, individuals accused me of things I didn't do. Inevitably, all these interactions forced me to face the truth. My marriage was over. As I grew to accept this reality, my finances, custody arrangements, and the well-being of my daughters plagued my heart. There is nothing good about divorce. Divorce forces you to make huge life decisions while struggling with deep, emotional rejection. So, naturally, looking in the mirror was the last thing I wanted to do.

Yet, there I stood, surrendering to the moment, and allowing myself to receive what God had for me. As the floodgates opened, my first instinct was to flee, but God insisted I stay in front of the mirror for at least fifteen minutes. So, I set a timer.

Friends let me tell you. Fifteen minutes feels like *forever* when you stand in front of a mirror looking at yourself!

At first glance, all I could see were the lumps, bumps, scars, and imperfections of my body. My flaws exposed, God encouraged me to look deeper, and look past the imperfections. Even though He had already proven himself to me, the biggest realization I had was how much my ability to trust fluctuated. Could I really count on anyone? Could I count on God?

Chapter 21 – Embrace

I don't have words to describe what happened next, but the longer I stood there, this sweet tenderness swept over me. Sensing His presence, I heard him speak kindness, even though His voice wasn't audible. Exhausted, I positioned myself to receive as Psalm 51:17 (NIV) came to mind: *The sacrifice you desire is a broken spirit. You will not reject a broken and repentant heart, O God.* Trying to see past my brokenness, I confessed the things I needed to turn from and the resentment I felt when others didn't turn. Could the God of the universe really desire the sacrifice of my broken spirit? Didn't I have the right to hang onto it?

Many questions came up during those fifteen minutes, but this particular question had a quick answer. YES! My brokenness was an offering which needed to be sacrificed. I didn't need it. I needed to be loved, to be heard, to be seen. Friends, when you hit rock bottom, any kind of validation feels like a lifeline.

First, God acknowledged the deep rejection I felt. He reminded me how my responses were reasonable, and whispered it was okay to lament to Him. As tears flowed, His words injected me like water to a thirsty soul. I will never forget the very first word I heard. It was my name. Susan. Hearing the God of the universe address me so personally healed a deep, dark hole inside. He said "Allow me to lead you. Let the dross rise to the surface so I can purify. Take one step at a time and follow me. I will take you to the room of grace."

As I entered the room, words of affirmation flowed. His gentle whispers included loving, intimate messages. He tenderly said: "Notice your arms; those are the arms you used to hug your friend when she was in pain. Notice your scar; that was how your beautiful daughter came into the world. Notice your breasts; they gave great nourishment to your children." Layers and layers of intimate discoveries were acknowledged. God's healing started with validation, ultimately satisfying some of the deepest needs I didn't know I had.

A Firm GRASP

As He affirmed me, we celebrated. The dark clouds and shadows of deep-rooted rejection left the room, never to return. Instead, light filled the room as tears of joy poured down my cheeks. As I saw Him smile at me, I was reminded that God is indeed president of my fan club. He is my safety net, my refuge.

As I experienced His love, I did the Spiritual Sigh. As I exhaled my burdens, and inhaled His presence, something changed. Like a scene from a movie, He softly reached out his hand and asked me to dance. As I took a firm grasp of His hand, He led me towards the dance floor. As music filled the room, I felt the waves of safety and serenity. As I experienced His presence, I couldn't resist feeling beautiful. All of this happened when I said yes to the dance!

My dear friends, as you read this, I hope you can visualize this intimate, spiritual scene. He noticed a fragile, wounded heart and gave me a glimpse of what's to come. One can only imagine what it will feel like to experience the full presence of God! What a day that will be!

Honestly, this moment was so special, I didn't feel the need to share it with anyone. Maybe there was part of me which thought others would view it as weird. My perspective changed when I read through Mary Magdalene's visit to the tomb after Jesus died. Grieving, she entered the tomb to see He was gone and became curious about where they took her Lord.

John 20:11-18 describes the scene: *"But Mary stood weeping outside the tomb, and as she wept, she stooped to look into the tomb. And she saw two angels in white, sitting where the body of Jesus had lain, one at the head and one at the feet. They said to her, 'Woman, why are you weeping?' She said to them, 'They have taken away my Lord, and I do not know where they have laid him.' Having said this, she turned around and saw Jesus standing, but she did not know that it was Jesus. Jesus said to her, 'Woman, why are you weeping? Whom are*

Chapter 21 – Embrace

you seeking?' Supposing him to be the gardener, she said to him, 'Sir, if you have carried him away, tell me where you have laid him, and I will take him away.' Jesus said to her, 'Mary.' She turned and said to him in Aramaic. 'Rabboni!(which means Teacher).' Jesus said to her, 'Do not cling to me, for I have not yet ascended to the Father; but go to my brothers and say to them, 'I am ascending to my Father and your Father, to my God and your God.' Mary Magdalene went and announced to the disciples, 'I have seen the Lord'—and that he had said these things to her."

As I picture this scene, I wonder what it would've been like for Mary. She didn't recognize Him at first, like many of us. That is, until He addressed her by name. Until He acknowledged her. Then she knew.

Perhaps you long to sense His presence in a more intimate way or would love to hear the God of the Universe say your name. Although my experience involved me, I learned it wasn't about me. It wasn't just about feeling beautiful again or being validated. Instead, by acknowledging Him and embracing His beauty, I was able to embrace mine. That's how mercy works.

Friends, I did nothing to deserve this experience, but I do know it was uniquely designed to meet my needs. You too, will experience Him in a unique way. Because of His Son, we all are invited to the dance! As God showered me with mercy, I discovered the peace mercy brings, because mercy lives, mercy gives, and mercy covers all of us. This mercy extends to my children, colleagues, friends, family, and yes, even my ex-husband. As Jehovah-Rapa, the God who heals, He knows the depths of my cry, but He also wants the sacrifice of my spirit, no matter how broken. Psalm 116:1-2 tells us: *"I love the LORD, because he has heard my voice and my pleas for mercy. Because he inclined his ear to me, therefore I will call on him as long as I live."*

A Firm GRASP

So, I invite you to accept His invitation. Go ahead and get a firm grasp on the hand of the one who loves you. Grasp onto the one who sees all facets. Regardless of our brokenness or our feelings of unworthiness, His cross says we are worth it. We are worth the price of His Son. Those fifteen minutes are an anchor for me when messages of rejection attempt to take over or I need the affirmation of a father. Those fifteen minutes are a constant reminder I am His masterpiece, even when betrayed or abused. Those fifteen minutes allowed me to embrace mercy, teaching me to shower myself and others in the same way.

Fifteen minutes can change you too.

As you position yourself to receive the healing powers of mercy, it may not mean standing in front of a mirror. God's invitation will be designed just for you. If it's anything like mine, it will turn out to be a painfully, wonderful adventure. As you receive His validation and watch His smile as He celebrates you, you will experience a peace swelling in your heart. As you get a firm grasp and say yes to the dance, your spirit will come alive. All you have to do is embrace and you'll discover your masterpiece.

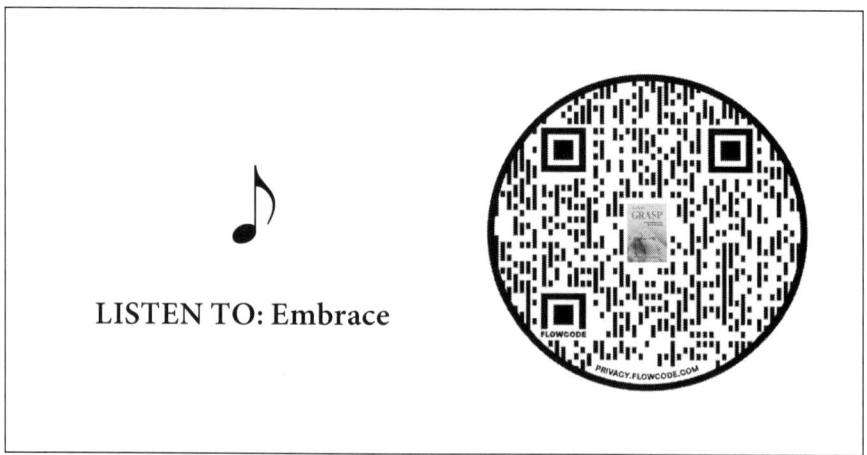

LISTEN TO: Embrace

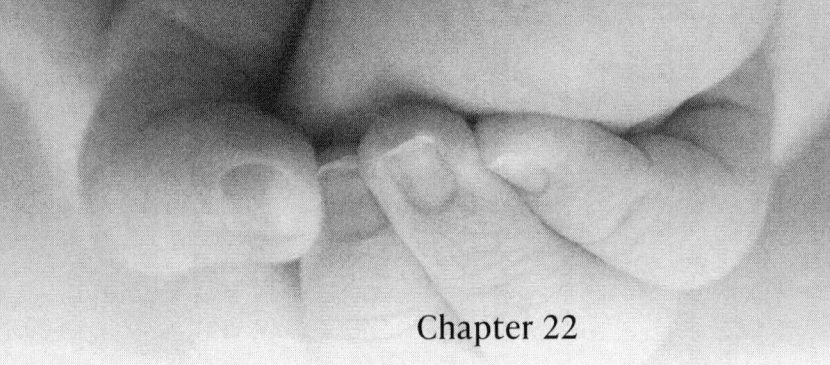

Chapter 22

MASPIECE

———————————— " ————————————

*"Create in me a clean heart, O God, and renew
a steadfast spirit within me. He has created us
anew in Christ Jesus, so we can do the
good things he planned for us long ago."*
—**Psalm 51:10**

I've never thought of myself as a masterpiece. If you're like me, instead of thinking of yourself as a work of art, you see every flaw. Blemishes, wrinkles, a broad nose, and extra weight contribute to my feelings of inadequacy. As I age, sometimes I look in the mirror and wonder who that person truly is. Aren't I still twenty-five? Friends, my perceptions are off.

A few years back, *Dove Soap* did a study. They produced a film entitled *Real Beauty Sketches*, which challenged perceptions. The study included women interviewed behind a screen, where they described themselves to an FBI-trained forensic artist who sketched their portrait. Later, the same artist drew another picture of the same woman, but this time, a stranger gave the description.

What happened? The sketches were undeniably different. Each of the women's self-descriptions depicted a plain, unflattering view. When describing themselves, the women exaggerated birthmarks, wrinkles, and facial structures. However, the stranger's descriptions did the opposite. They enhanced their positive characteristics without exaggerating their flaws. What did it prove? That our perceptions are off. We don't see our own beauty.

Misconceptions

Misconceptions of ourselves aren't limited to the way we look. Sometimes we restrict ourselves based on overt talents or achievements. We believe messages from our deficient fan club or what the Hall of Shame says about us. Statements like "You're worthless, you'll never be good enough," or "You are a failure and will never amount to anything," radiate our senses. Our perspective continues to get skewed when we compare. It's as if we think an apple and orange are the same.

In Ephesians 2:10, Paul wrote, *"We are His workmanship, created in Christ Jesus for good works, which God prepared beforehand that we should walk in them."* The original Greek word for workmanship is *poiema*, literally meaning *a poem or a work of art*. Friends, you are God's work of art. He put considerable thought into the rhyme and rhythm of your life. Psalms 139 tells us that He knows every hair upon your head and knows what you are going to say even before you say it. He knows you and intimately sees you. He sees your skin color, gender, family placement, abilities, and flaws.

As an artist, God put more detail into creating you than many other artists did creating their masterpieces. Think about the time it took for Beethoven to write nine symphonies or for Michelangelo to paint the Sistine Chapel ceiling. Your Creator gave more attention to the details in crafting you than Robert Frost did on all his poems

Chapter 22 – Masterpiece

combined. Our bodies in and of themselves are an amazing group of systems. We are His workmanship! Do you believe it? Can you receive it?

You don't have to have an intimate experience like I did to feel God's presence. God carefully placed each eyelash. He lined up each tooth precisely so no one else would have your smile. Though we have the same parts, no two people share the same DNA. God takes pleasure in your uniqueness because He made you. But you are so much more than just how you look.

Remember the expression 'your eyes are the window to your soul'? Behind that outward package is the real you—a unique package of personality traits, talents, backgrounds, experiences, and spiritual gifts—the facet you present to the world.

When your Father looks at you, as a believer in Jesus Christ, what does He see? He sees beauty and greatness. Although He is completely aware of your sin and shame, His mercy tells us that is no longer an issue. "I don't care what others say about you. You are my priceless work of art, full of divine potential. I created you to do things nobody else can do in this entire world."

Simply put, to be a masterpiece means you are a piece of the Master.

The Creator

As a God who celebrates uniqueness, He celebrates you. As a creator, He created over 200 dog breeds, over 60,000 species of trees, and over 250,000 flowers. Some are larger, some bloom for a short time, each bearing its own leaves, colors, and life span. God is diverse. Friends, God affirms you through your uniqueness. Every day, He is creating masterpieces.

Webster's Dictionary defines masterpieces as "a work of outstanding artistry, skill, or workmanship." Notice this definition emphasizes that it's a work. The implication is that in order for the work to exist, a creator was necessary. Could that mean being a masterpiece isn't about you or how you feel about yourself, but about WHO made you?

As we discovered in the chapter called *Facets*, each of us has our own perspective. Our experiences, fan club, frame, and self-awareness skills influence the way we view the world. But, dear reader, as a piece of the Master, this means He designed you—all of you—to reflect a piece of Him…a facet cleverly designed to radiate His presence to those around you.

The how

So how do we radiate His presence? By catching the light. We do this through our presence, connection, gifts, sphere of influence, and storytelling.

First, we catch the light by simply being us, His creation. Our very **presence** reflects God because the Holy Spirit lives in us. Think of the times you are experiencing beautiful scenery. Don't you get a glimpse of God? One can't help but see how unique and thoughtful nature is. We can appreciate God through His beautiful sunsets, beaches, and mountains. We can hear Him in the sound of a waterfall, the feel of the wind, or the purity of fresh fallen snow. Each mountain is a piece of Him—not all of Him, but a piece of Him, reflecting a part of His essence. When I lived in Colorado, the mountains reminded me of the power and strength of God. So why do we find it difficult to embrace *ourselves* as a part of Him?

God's creation takes up space. Our space is our inalienable right to life. Take some time to look in the mirror and embrace what God said when He created you and said, "and it was good." You occupy space.

Chapter 22 – Masterpiece

You might ask, "So are you saying that just by existing, I reflect the Master?" Yes!

That's not all, however. We reflect God when we are **connected** to the Holy Spirit. This is when the fruit of the Spirit emerges as love, joy, peace, patience, kindness, goodness, grace, gentleness, and self-control. Friends, *all* of these pieces of Him look good on you! As we surrender to the Spirit, we reflect Him. Our facet shines for Him. Psalm 34:5 (NIV) tells us, *"Those who look to him are radiant: faces covered with no shame."*

But there's more. Each of us has a unique package of **gifts**. We are given human gifts, namely talents, that are most likely based on our genetic structure or family placement. Some are given a knack for math, strategy, or athleticism. Some are given financial resources or artistic talent. All human gifts have limitations, but each of us has a package unique to us. For example, I'm not talented enough, nor do I have the experience or background to be an Olympic ice skater; but I can write a song, play the clarinet, lay counsel, and write. Maybe you are a good problem solver or have a great sense of humor. All are gifts designed to glorify Him, wrapped in mercy.

Finally, the best gifts are the spiritual ones, which include discernment, administration, exhortation, faith, giving, healing, helps, prophecy, teaching, hospitality, wisdom, service, tongues, and—you guessed it—mercy. Each of us is given at least one of these gifts at salvation. As we grow, we may receive others. All these gifts are supported through our connection to the Holy Spirit. We cannot exercise these gifts without God. Romans 11:29-32 explains: *"For the gifts and the calling of God are irrevocable. For just as you were at one time disobedient to God but now have received mercy because of their disobedience, so they too have now been disobedient in order that by the mercy shown to you they also may now receive mercy. For God has consigned all to disobedience, that he may have mercy on all."*

As we exercise the gifts of the spirit, something special happens. Although God can use our overt talent, it's the spiritual gifts we can't explain. When I am surrendered to the Spirit, amazing things happen way beyond my package of human talents.

Where do we exercise our gifts? In our **sphere of influence**. For example, if my human gifts and family placement led me to the ice-skating world, that would be my sphere of influence. In my sphere, I can display the fruit of the spirit and use my spiritual gifts to spread the message of mercy. Your sphere of influence is whoever is in front of you—and it is unique to you. Whether a colleague, a student, or the person scheduling your dentist appointment, you have a sphere of influence that no one else taps into exactly the way you do.

Lastly, we reflect Him by **telling our story**. Our story, our experiences, and our testimony can bring comfort and encouragement to others. Each story of redemption needs to be shared. By sharing how God redeemed us, we see how God has validated us when others didn't. We take notice…of God…of others…of ourselves. Your story is part of your masterpiece package and needs to be told. It's not a suggestion; God actually commanded us to go and tell!

Many people get caught up about how they are going to tell their story. They wonder whether they need to write a book, be a preacher or teacher, or write a song. They wonder if it means they have to be in ministry full time or quit their job to tell their story or activate their gifts. Yes, and yes. Maybe your masterpiece package includes the gift of speaking or writing, so yes, you will gravitate towards speaking or writing. Perhaps you have the gift of compassion. Can you be compassionate as you speak or write, or can you be just as compassionate when you give up your place in line at the grocery store? Each time you meet another person, you are telling your unique story of redemption through your masterpiece package. No one else can reflect Him the same way you can.

John Piper said in his book, *Don't Waste Your Life*, "God created me—and you—to live with a single, all-embracing, all-transforming passion—namely, a passion to glorify God by enjoying and displaying His supreme excellence in all the spheres of life."

Mercy sees

How do we glorify God? Does it matter what season of life we are in or what roles we serve? Are we part of a small group or a greeter at church? Do we teach Sunday school or sing on the worship team? Mercy sees us in whatever sphere God has placed us.

Ray Boltz talks about the impact we have on others in his song "Thank You for Giving to the Lord." Friends, we don't always know the impact our presence, the fruit of the Spirits, our gifts, or our story has on others in our sphere of influence. As we live in mercy mode, we radiate mercy to others. Mercy allows us to see others. This may include being vulnerable enough to let the dross in our lives bubble towards the surface to radiate God's mercy. William Secker said, "Until we taste the bitterness of our own misery, we will never relish the sweetness of God's mercy. Until we see how foul our sins have made us, we will never pay our tribute of praise to Christ for washing us…If you would know the heart of your sin, then you must know the sins of your heart!"

Being a masterpiece doesn't mean perfection. It doesn't mean you don't have issues to work through. But as a piece of the Master, you reflect a facet of him.

Take a moment to picture this. Arriving in heaven, can you see all of our facets shining simultaneously? What a glorious day that will be! So, get out your paintbrush and start painting. We need to see a glimpse of heaven here. Don't wait for someone else to validate your presence, connection, gifts, sphere of influence, or story. God already did, and He's waiting to celebrate you!

A Firm GRASP

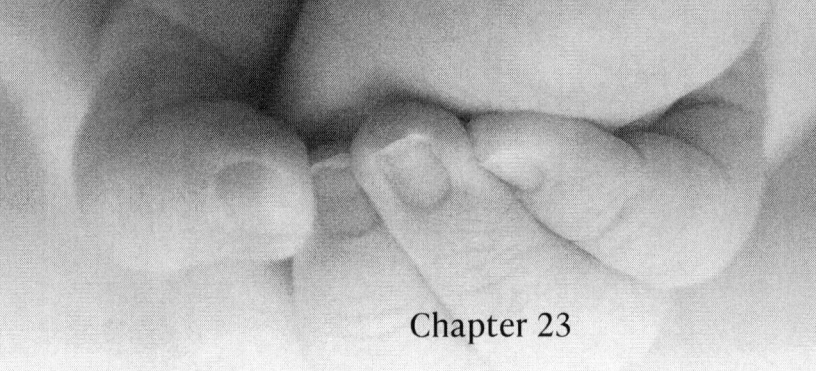

Chapter 23

THE MASTER

――――――――――― " ―――――――――――

*God's mercy is so great that you may sooner
drain the sea of its water, or deprive the sun of
its light, or make space too narrow than
diminish the great mercy of God.*
—**Charles Spurgeon**

Music is one of my best friends. Music has been there for me during moments of grief, break-ups, and unrequited love. As my career, it has been a source of livelihood. I have had the honor of performing some of the best classical masterpieces. Talent has taught me so much about validation and affirmation. I've become aware how the trap of comparison makes me feel inadequate and how applause is fleeting. I discovered how to learn from others who were more advanced than I without feeling unworthy. God showed me the power of the lament through songwriting. During those darkest times, where I was unsure about life, seeking out broken cisterns, and questioning God, the music seemed to be my closest friend. Sometimes, lyrics of a song understood me to my core. What a gift.

During one of those thought-provoking seasons, I discovered a song made famous by Bob Dylan, *"Gotta Serve Somebody."* This song appeared just when I was struggling with my identity. The song describes individuals and their various roles in life. The overall message is that no matter who we are, we serve somebody. When all is said and done, we do have a Master. The song encouraged me to begin asking myself new questions: *who* do I serve? *why* do I serve? *how* do I serve?

For those of us who struggle because we have not been validated or affirmed, the *how* we serve rises to the surface. We wonder what roles we play, what status we have in the church or ministry, or how others will notice us. Our quest to be noticed, and perhaps our ability to serve, cannot be quenched without understanding our dross and receiving mercy. Surrendering our idols, being available to serve in secret, with love, is our response to that mercy.

Surrendering Idols

How we serve cannot be discussed without understanding *who* we serve.

My answer to the *who* question varied during different seasons of my life. At first, I acted like my masterpiece was mine to do with as I pleased. Other times, because it was my identity, I served music and the affirmation which came with it. When I married and had children, I served my family. In all of these stages of life, without realizing it, I chose *who* I was going to serve. When my focus was strictly on others, yes, there were moments of happiness. But I wouldn't say I was satisfied because my cistern wasn't full. I kept needing more.

Jesus, our Master, invites us to understand why we aren't satisfied. In Matthew 6:24, He tells us, *"No servant can serve two masters: for either he will hate the one and love the other; or else he will hold to one and despise the other. You cannot serve God and money."*

In this passage, Jesus uses money to highlight the biggest obstacle we have: picking one master. Your "money" could be your family, job, or ministry. Perhaps it's your marriage, your sports, or stimulants. Whatever gets put before The Master is an idol. Pastor Jack Magruder, a guest on THE NOTICE podcast explains a good way to assess if something else is your master. "Ask yourself two questions: What would you do if that something or someone was taken from you? How do you react if someone challenges your mindset about that someone or something?" Once we surrender our idols, we make ourselves available, to serve in secret, with love.

Being available

Many of us fight the very idea of a master or that we need to be available or accountable to someone else. To have a master suggests we may be slaves, with someone else getting all the glory. This allows us to feel justified to fight our boss, our pastor, or even our president, because they may be unreasonable or unfair, or they don't appreciate or affirm us. In our pride, we 'know' there is a better way of doing things. As Monica Lewinsky said: "I am the boss of me." Yet, we weren't designed to be the master of our lives.

The word *Master* is often translated *lord* and denotes the owner or master of a servant or slave. During biblical times, the master of the house was the ruler, the taskmaster, the head or chief. He made decisions for the servants of the house.

The parable of the vineyard workers in Matthew 20:1-16 provides an interesting application for us. In this parable, the master of the vineyard hired workers five times during the day. He selected when the workers started and how many hours they would work. The first shift began at 6 a.m. At 9 a.m., he returned to call more workers and agreed to pay them "whatever is right." He did the same at noon and 3 p.m. At 5 p.m., he went out to hire more workers.

At what was probably sunset, the master came to pay everyone. Even though all the workers clocked in at different times, the master paid everyone the same wage. One can only imagine the uproar.

The 6 a.m. workers didn't think the master was fair. Compared to the others who all began later, these workers felt they should have received more pay. However, they didn't look at the workers' hearts as the master did. Were the 5 p.m. workers stubborn or lazy? No. But they were available. In God's kingdom, servants aren't straining to be validated or affirmed. They are simply available.

In Secret

One of the best ways we can serve is to be available. But what if we allow ourselves to be available, and no one notices? Steven Furtick, Pastor of Elevation Church, in his sermon *You Can't Let Others Control You*, talks about this other "how": "There is no worse feeling than that of invisibility. You know, when you are doing your very best and it goes unrecognized, it makes it kinda hard to want to keep doing it. And when you feel unseen, especially by the people whose attention and approval you crave the most, it can create a compulsion in your life to start doing things that are not even really consistent with your character in order to receive from people a confirmation that can be taken away just as easily as it was given. But we are not citizens of this kingdom which celebrates and compliments all the things that are seen. We are citizens of a kingdom where Jesus says things like this: When you do something in secret, your Father sees it, and He will reward you according to what He sees. So my message is, if you have felt unappreciated, uncelebrated, unnoticed, and insignificant in this kingdom, what is unseen is often what is most significant."

Matthew 6:3-6 tells us, *"But when you give to the needy, do not let your left hand know what your right hand is doing, so that your giving may be in secret. And your Father who sees in secret will reward you. And when you pray, you must not be like the hypocrites. For they love to stand and pray in the synagogues and at the street corners, that they may be seen by others. Truly, I say to you, they have received their reward. But when you pray, go into your room and shut the door and pray to your Father who is in secret. And your Father who sees in secret will reward you."*

In Love

Surrendering our idols, being available and serving in secret, combined with love, is a winning combination. As part of love, we acknowledge and affirm each other.

Jean Vainer, the founder of L'Arche, an international network of 147 communities in thirty-five countries for persons with mental and physical disabilities, discovered a new layer of love. While living in France, his life work became clear when he observed government-sponsored psychiatric hospitals. He considered those institutionalized as the most oppressed of individuals. So, he invited two men from the hospital to live with him in a small village to understand better their needs. Here's what he discovered.

"Living with men and women with mental disabilities has helped me to discover what it means to live in communion with someone. To be in communion means to be with someone...accepting people just as they are, with all their limits and inner pain, but also with their gifts and their beauty...to see the beauty inside of all the pain. To love someone is not first of all to do things for them, but to reveal to them their beauty and value, to say to them through our attitude: "You are beautiful. You are important. I trust you. You can trust yourself."

In order to be ready to serve, we have to receive the validation we get from God so we can in turn, validate others. But we need to know who The Master really is.

Belonging

As a piece of the Master, you *do* belong to someone—the Master—the almighty God. Friends, let me tell you about this Master. He is like no other.

God is more than we can ever think or imagine. His love, mercy, justice, power, omnipresence, and sovereignty are undisputable. But He is also dichotomous, just like us. He understands the seesaw. Philippians 2:5-8 further explains the kind of Master we have: *"Having this mind among yourselves, which is yours in Christ Jesus, who, though he was in the form of God, did not count equality with God a thing to be grasped, but emptied himself, by taking the form of a servant, being born in the likeness of men. And being found in human form, he humbled himself by becoming obedient to the point of death, even death on a cross."*

To have a firm grasp means to let go of wanting to be your own master and get a firm grasp on *the* Master. It means being comfortable with feeling unworthy and worth it simultaneously. It means accepting the fact that mercy fulfills our need for validation and affirmation. So, go ahead, and grab His hand.

Mercy rules

Throughout this book, we have defined our need for validation and affirmation as a basic human need. We've concluded that it is not wrong or evil to desire it, but it can get out of control. Our enemy, Satan, tempts us in this area because he has an insatiable appetite to be celebrated, worshipped even. He didn't think being a piece of the Master was enough. He didn't understand what it meant to have a firm grasp.

Many questions are posed in this book, but here are some concluding ones to consider: *Who* will you grasp onto? *How* will you serve? *Why* will you serve?

Chapter 23 – The Master

As we discussed in the previous chapter, we were designed to paint our masterpiece, using our gifts in whatever sphere of influence we are placed. This could be the person waiting on you at a restaurant or emailing you with a request. Maybe it's the customer you serve at work, the person for whom you are writing a book, or the child you are raising. God's calling on our life is to paint that masterpiece, where your divine space exists. Express yourself by living in mercy mode—acknowledging (validating) someone else's right to their perspective or experience and celebrating (affirming) them when you agree. Now that we better understand the how, and we understand the who, *why* do we serve?

It all gets back to God. We serve because of *who* God is and how He has brought us into relationship with Him. We serve because we have received the mercy of God. 2 Peter 1:10 says: *Once you were not a people, but now you are God's people; once you had not received mercy, but now you have received mercy.*

My dear reader, it's always about the Gospel. The Gospel's message is wrapped in mercy. Mercy reminds us that although we deserve punishment for our sins, God's work on the cross takes the punishment for us. This means we no longer have to be a slave to our feelings of unworthiness or being good enough. We recognize that we are both worthy and worth it simultaneously. We look for opportunities to validate and affirm the message of the Gospel and encourage others to come with us to our true country.

In *Mere Christianity*[1], C.S. Lewis says: "Creatures are not born with desires unless satisfaction for those desires exists. A baby feels hunger: well, there is such a thing as food. A duckling wants to swim: well, there is such a thing as water. Men feel sexual desire: well, there

---

[1] *Mere Christianity* by CS Lewis © copyright CS Lewis Pte Ltd 1942, 1943, 1944 1952. Used with permission.

is such a thing as sex. If I find in myself a desire which no experience in this world can satisfy, the most probable explanation is that I was made for another world. If none of my earthly pleasures satisfy it, that does not prove that the universe is a fraud. Probably earthly pleasures were never meant to satisfy it, but only to arouse it, to suggest the real thing. If that is so, I must take care, on the one hand, never to despise, or to be unthankful for, these earthly blessings, and on the other, never to mistake them for the something else of which they are only a kind of copy, or echo, or mirage. I must keep alive in myself the desire for my true country, which I shall not find till after death; I must never let it get snowed under or turned aside; I must make it the main object of life to press on to that country and to help others to do the same."

2 Timothy 2:20-21 reminds us, *"Now in a great house there are not only vessels of gold and silver but also of wood and clay, some for honorable use, some for dishonorable. Therefore, if anyone cleanses himself from what is dishonorable, he will be a vessel for honorable use, set apart as holy, useful to the Master of the house, ready for every good work."*

My friends, as you get a firm grasp, may you position yourself to receive the validation and affirmation that comes from mercy. May self-awareness allow you to face your dross and surrender your idols. As you do, your story, your piece of the Master, becomes a masterpiece, ready and available to serve Him, in secret, and in love. May God have mercy on us all.

LISTEN TO: Mercy Prayer

SOAKING SESSION
for personal reflection

Dear readers,

The journey towards self-awareness this book encourages is a crucial step to getting a firm grasp. Like you, I've struggled to understand the complexities and simplicity of mercy. Yet, God gives us gifts along the way to help us process. I've been blessed to have music be one of those gifts.

So, it seemed fitting to share the music God gave me during my journey with you. Please take a few minutes to "soak" up the reflective music and quotes from the book. Yes, it's me the author, performing the clarinet. Some of the instrumental arrangements are mine, and although the songs were written by me, I've been blessed to have others sing them. You are invited to take some time to process all God has for you. May He shower you with His mercy in an unforgettable way.

Access to the *A Firm Grasp* Soaking Session can be found here:
https://susankhoekstra.com/songs

Life - Line Chart

The Life -Line Chart is a tool that can be used in a number of ways. It is especially helpful as you take a strong look at your dross, your frame, how you've cramped yourself, and the Hall of Shame. But it is also helpful to understand what God has done in the process. Be sure to use this tool with the assistance of a professional or lay counselor.

Validation and Affirmation QUIZES

You can find access to the Validation and Affirmation quizzes here:
https://susankhoekstra.com/affirm-grasp

REFLECTIVE QUESTIONS
for personal and small group study

Chapter 1 – The Handshake

Satan tried to get Jesus to question who he was. How have you been tempted in this area?

_____
_____
_____
_____
_____

Discuss a time when you felt validated. (Based on the new definitions)

_____
_____
_____
_____
_____

Discuss a time when you felt affirmed. (Based on the new definitions)

_____
_____
_____
_____
_____

Chapter 2 – Give and take

How do you respond when you are rejected?

Do you ever feel like you are hypervigilant? Have you noticed that in others?

What things, persons, or attitudes do you give to God and then take back?

Chapter 3 – Be Still

Describe the times you sensed God's presence.

_____
_____
_____
_____
_____

Where do you go to cultivate silence?

_____
_____
_____
_____
_____

How does understanding surrender help us be still?

_____
_____
_____
_____
_____
_____
_____
_____

Chapter 4 – A Star is Born

Describe a time that you met a star

_____
_____
_____
_____
_____
_____

What gifts do you have that are uniquely you?

_____
_____
_____
_____
_____
_____
_____
_____

Describe your sphere of influence

_____
_____
_____
_____
_____
_____
_____

Chapter 5 – The Fan Club

Was your fan club adequate or faulty?

_____
_____
_____
_____
_____
_____

Did you feel validated or affirmed?

_____
_____
_____
_____
_____
_____

What ways does God validate you?

_____
_____
_____
_____
_____
_____

Chapter 6 – Facets

What facet is uniquely yours?

_____
_____
_____
_____
_____
_____

How do you feel when someone validates your facet? How do you feel when they don't?

_____
_____
_____
_____
_____

How can your facet shine for Jesus?

_____
_____
_____
_____
_____
_____
_____

Chapter 7 – The Frame

After doing your Life-Line Chart, what have your discovered about your frame?

_____
_____
_____
_____
_____
_____
_____
_____

Which parts of your frame have sent you painful messages? Which have sent you validating or affirming messages?

_____
_____
_____
_____
_____
_____
_____
_____
_____

Chapter 8 – Enter the Hall

What sins have you committed that make you feel shame?

_____
_____
_____
_____
_____
_____
_____
_____
_____

What sins have been committed against you that make you feel shame?

_____
_____
_____
_____
_____
_____
_____
_____
_____

Share your shame with someone.

Chapter 9 – The Vow

Have you made a vow?

How has that vow affected your actions and beliefs?

How does mercy change your view?

Chapter 10 – The Trap

What makes you feel inadequate? Who makes you feel inadequate?

_____
_____
_____
_____
_____

Which of the Bible characters could you relate to the most?

_____
_____
_____
_____
_____
_____

Remember, persist, acknowledge, or obey – Which one do you struggle with?

_____
_____
_____
_____
_____

Chapter 11 – CRAMPS

Which of the following do you tend to gravitate to?
Catastrophe | Resentment | Affirmation | Manipulation | Performance | Striving

_____
_____

How does being aware of your cramps help your response to life happenings or sin?

_____
_____
_____
_____
_____
_____
_____
_____
_____
_____
_____
_____
_____
_____
_____

Chapter 12 – I-dentity

What ways have you searched for your identity? Did it satisfy?

_____
_____
_____
_____
_____

What messages do you believe about yourself?

_____
_____
_____
_____
_____

What would it feel like to come to accept your unworthiness? How would your life change?

_____
_____
_____
_____
_____
_____
_____

Reflective Questions

Chapter 13 – The Seesaw

What areas of your life are you seeking balance?

_____
_____
_____
_____
_____

Which of the opposites do you struggle with the most?

_____
_____
_____
_____
_____

How does becoming aware of our seesaw change our perspective on balance?

_____
_____
_____
_____
_____

Chapter 14 – Offense or Defense

How do you respond when someone doesn't agree with you?

_____
_____
_____
_____
_____

How do you respond when someone gives you feedback?

_____
_____
_____
_____
_____

How do you respond when someone challenges things in your life that are important to you?

_____
_____
_____
_____
_____

Chapter 15 – The Why

Tell about a time you did something good but for the wrong reasons.

_____
_____
_____
_____
_____
_____

Tell about a time you did something bad, but your intentions were good

_____
_____
_____
_____
_____

Think about a situation where you aren't aware of your "why" and go through the check your motive section.

_____
_____
_____
_____
_____
_____

Chapter 16 – Selfies

Take a look at the Self List. Is there one you gravitate to more than others?

_____
_____
_____

How is being self-aware different than self-esteem?

_____
_____
_____
_____
_____

Discuss the difference between being self-aware and selfish.

_____
_____
_____
_____
_____
_____
_____
_____

Chapter 17 – Who's listening?

Discuss the various listening styles. Which one is your go to?
_____
_____
_____
_____
_____
_____

What new methods could you try to become a better listener?
_____
_____
_____
_____
_____
_____

What do you expect from others when you complain?
_____
_____
_____
_____
_____
_____
_____
_____

Chapter 18 – Treat Yourself

Discuss the difference between self-care and self-indulgence
_____
_____
_____
_____
_____

What human limitations do you struggle to acknowledge or accept?
_____
_____
_____
_____
_____
_____

How does understanding that sin makes you unworthy change your self-awareness?
_____
_____
_____
_____
_____
_____
_____
_____

Chapter 19 – Mercy Mode

What ways have you seen others extend mercy to you?

_____
_____
_____
_____
_____
_____

Discuss what Jesus was saying when He said *"Go and learn what this means: 'I desire mercy, and not sacrifice.'*

_____
_____
_____
_____
_____
_____

What is keeping you from getting a firm grasp on God's mercy?

_____
_____
_____
_____
_____
_____

Chapter 20 – Safety Net

What areas of your life leave you feeling unsafe?

_____
_____
_____
_____
_____
_____

What does it take for you to feel safe enough to be authentic?

_____
_____
_____
_____
_____
_____
_____
_____
_____

How does telling your story benefit you, others, God?

_____
_____
_____
_____
_____
_____
_____

Chapter 21 – Embrace

How does it feel to be involved in someone else's vulnerable story?

_____
_____
_____
_____
_____
_____
_____

How do you feel when you look in the mirror?

_____
_____
_____
_____
_____
_____
_____

What needs to change in order to embrace how God sees you?

_____
_____
_____
_____
_____
_____
_____

Chapter 22 – Masterpiece

What misconceptions do you have about yourself?

_____
_____
_____
_____
_____

How does mercy change your perspective of yourself, of others, of God?

_____
_____
_____
_____
_____

Discuss the ways everyone's facets (pieces of the Master) will shine when we see Jesus.

_____
_____
_____
_____
_____
_____

Chapter 23 – The Master

What ways do you struggle with wanting to be your own master?

_____
_____
_____
_____

Discuss the challenges of surrendering idols, being available, serving in secret and serving in love.

_____
_____
_____
_____
_____
_____

What is the recipe for getting our validation and affirmation needs met?

_____
_____
_____
_____

Wondering if you really have a validation deficit? Take this quiz: **https://susankhoekstra.com/affirm-grasp**

Do you ever feel invisible or unheard? Do you find yourself grasping onto words of affirmation like a lifeline? Join host Susan Hoekstra on THE NOTICE, a podcast which explores our need to be noticed through biblical musings and unique stories from special guests. Experience relevant topics and encouragement as we take notice of how the God of mercy satisfies.

thenotice.podbean.com

COMING SOON...
A Firm GRASP Webinars

Want to learn how to give and receive validation and affirmation more authentically?
Visit Susan's website for upcoming webinars designed especially for:

Teachers | Parents and Grandparents
The father-less | Creatives | Worship Leaders
Lay Counselors | Ministry Leaders

A Firm GRASP *e-devotional*

www.susankhoekstra.com

About the Author

Susan Hoekstra started *A Firm GRASP Ministries* to encourage others to gain a firm grasp on God's mercy, leading them to notice the way God notices.

Born into Polish-Catholic heritage and raised in the streets of Detroit, Susan Hoekstra, at the age of ten, experienced the loss of her father. At age thirteen, she came to a saving faith in Jesus at a local youth group, but also dreamed of leaving her low socio-economic background and becoming a professional clarinetist. She did it. She earned music scholarships and degrees, performing and teaching at the college level. She also held high profile positions in arts administration while raising two daughters.

From a distance, music appeared to satisfy her need to be noticed until her professional dreams didn't come true in the way she hoped, and her marriage shattered. The twists and turns of her spiritual transformation included financial insecurity, sexual abuse, adultery, family addictions, violence, divorce, the death of both parents, cancer, and a long list of heartaches. Her circumstances left her feeling unseen and ignored, believing she didn't have a fan club to give her the validation she needed.

Yet, God kept noticing her, kept pursuing her. He brought people into her life that saw her heartache as a temporary condition and introduced her to the mercy of God. Getting a firm grasp on God's mercy allowed her to look at herself and others through new eyes. Her determination to discover "who she is" resulted in discovering "whose she is."

Throughout this transformation, she began songwriting, leading small groups, teaching bible studies, speaking at women's retreats, writing, and lay counseling. She has been featured in *Just Between Us* magazine and *Christian Devotions*. She is host of THE NOTICE - God stories live, and THE NOTICE podcast. Her book *A Firm GRASP - Feeling validated in a notice-me world* is her first book. Sharing her diverse testimony and encouraging others towards a deeper understanding of God's mercy is her passion.

Should you want to invite Susan to speak at your conference, retreat, or offer a webinar to your small group or women's ministry, please contact her at **susan@susankhoekstra.com**

Susan is an experienced lay counselor and offers one-on-one discipleship sessions. You can sign up for a session by visiting her website.

www.susankhoekstra.com

Made in the USA
Columbia, SC
04 June 2021